A SELECTED BIBLIOGRAPHY
OF UTAH ARCHEOLOGY

Number 102   1979

A SELECTED BIBLIOGRAPHY
OF UTAH ARCHEOLOGY

by

Alan R. Schroedl

UNIVERSITY OF UTAH

ANTHROPOLOGICAL PAPERS

JESSE D. JENNINGS, EDITOR

University of Utah Press
Salt Lake City, Utah

ISBN 0-87480-141-9

CONTENTS

PREFACE

This bibliography results from a project undertaken by Alan R. Schroedl at the time he was an advanced graduate student at the University of Utah. As he left before it was completed, the task fell to several assistants. I therefore acknowledge with appreciation the help of Sharon Arnold, Dorothy Sammons, Barbara Jennings, and Marilyn Joress, who verified all titles (except in a few instances where this was impossible). Dorothy Sammons also typed the final copy which is reproduced here.

To make this bibliography available thirty years after the current program in intensive archeological research in Utah was initiated is a great personal pleasure for me. The dominant names in this bibliography since 1950 are those of students of the Department of Anthropology, which provides an index, perhaps, to the success of the twin objectives of the archeological program at the University: the advancement of knowledge, and the training of students through research opportunity.

The advancement in knowledge may be measured by comparing this bibliography with the one Elmer Smith prepared in 1950. Smith's bibliography lists about 150 titles, including ethnographic works. Thirty years later, this partial bibliography, with titles limited to archeology, numbers over 1000 entries. Admittedly, progress is not always measured by the numbers, which is to confess that some of the recent titles in this volume may border on the trivial. Most, however, are substantive contributions. In view of the fact that the literature pertaining to Utah prehistory has increased many-fold, this bibliography will, it is hoped, become a standard reference for younger students and for those who, for any reason, develop an interest in the details of Utah prehistory.

Jesse D. Jennings
Editor
June 1978

INTRODUCTION

Utah has been the scene of archeological investigations for more than 80 years. Since the 1890's, perhaps a thousand different publications have appeared as a result of these investigations. The quantity of information that is being published on Utah archeology seems to be growing at an exponential rate. In the spring of 1977, Professor Jesse D. Jennings asked me to compile a preliminary bibliography on Utah archeology while it was still a manageable task. The result of my compilation, the 1021 sources listed here, is the first published bibliography on Utah archeology.

I have collected these sources from the bibliographies of numerous books, articles, and reports; most of the sources have been cited at least once in one or another of the publications. Given this method of compilation, I am sure that there are a number of published sources on Utah archeology that I have missed but which should have been included in this bibliography. Except those citations which were not immediately available (marked with an asterisk), all items in this bibliography have been checked against the original sources to insure correct volume number, page number, spelling, etc.

The usefulness of this bibliography to serious archeological researchers is dependent upon my explanation of how I selected sources for inclusion. My primary criterion was that the source have some substantive content and contribute directly to the corpus of scientific archeological data for the state of Utah. The sources listed here include full-length books, serials, journal articles, theses and dissertations, manuscripts on file, contract and government reports, and cover a wide range of archeological topics such as survey reports, site reports, theoretical discussions, book reviews, comments and debates, artifacts reports, methodological papers, etc. I have deliberately excluded popular articles, newspaper accounts, "sensational" reports, and numerous broad general interest sources. Occasionally there are some early sources that I have included because of their historical significance in the development of Utah archeology.

In compiling these sources, I have tried to be all inclusive (within the selection criteria). However, there are undoubtedly omissions, particularly in sources dealing with contract archeology within the state of Utah. Numerous private companies and institutions (both from Utah and from other states) have conducted surveys and excavations in Utah which were reported directly to the designated private corporations and federal agencies. When I was aware of these reports they were cited, but I am sure many have been completed and submitted that I did not know about.

In order to underscore the preliminary nature of this bibliography, I must point out that working within the artifical political boundary of the state of Utah, although an easy means of delimiting the domain of possible sources, tends to obscure important cultural relationships in the archeological record. An unwary user might come to believe that the Fremont in Utah is different from the Fremont in Colorado or Nevada, or that the Anasazi in southeastern Utah differs significantly from the prehistoric Pueblo populations in the bordering states. Unfortunately, too much of the archeological literature in the western region is delineated by modern political boundaries rather than by archeological culture areas. I hope, then, that this bibliography serves as a basis for more detailed annotated bibliographies of the region that will be developed by different selection criteria, such as archeological culture areas, or chronological periods or even prominent geographical regions. Of course, any of these suggested formats for a bibliography has its own associated problems. Perhaps a feasible and economical alternative would be to develop an annotated bibliography cross-referenced according to each of these schemes and stored and maintained in a computer data file that could be easily and periodically updated. The compiling of this bibliography was done with note cards and sorted by hand. If done on a computer, it would be no additional task to list for a particular region all excavated sites, perhaps by components, with their primary published references.

In compiling these sources, I have relied heavily on the University of Utah Anthropological Papers, Antiquities Section Selected Papers, and Utah Archeology: A Newsletter. But researchers should be aware that numerous other journals and series exist in the intermountain region that often contain information pertinent to Utah archeology. Most of the major ones are listed below:

Arizona State Department of Anthropology, Anthropological Research Papers

Denver Museum of Natural History Popular Series

Desert Research Institute Technical Report Series, Social Sciences and Humanities

Idaho State University Museum Occasional Papers

Kiva

The Masterkey

Museum of Northern Arizona, Museum Notes, Bulletins, Technical Series, Ceramic Series

Nevada Archeological Survey Reporter

Nevada State Museum Anthropological Papers

Plateau

Southwestern Lore

Tebiwa

University of Arizona Anthropological Papers

University of Colorado Studies, Series in Anthropology

University of Idaho Anthropological Monographs

University of Northern Colorado Museum of Anthropology, Miscellaneous Series, and Occasional Publications in Anthropology: Archeology Series

I hope this discussion of my procedures for compiling the bibliography and my suggestions for more useful bibliographies will be of use to all regional scholars and researchers interested in the prehistory of the area.

Finally, I would like to acknowledge Professor Jesse D. Jennings for giving me the opportunity to compile this bibliography. Thanks are also due to those assistants who have carried it through the onerous clerical details to its completion.

Alan R. Schroedl
June 1978

A SELECTED BIBLIOGRAPHY
OF UTAH ARCHEOLOGY

BIBLIOGRAPHY

ABEL, LELAND J.

1955   Pottery Types of the South-
        west, Wares 5A, 10A, 10B,
        12A San Juan Red Ware, Mesa
        Verde Gray and White Ware,
        San Juan White Ware. Museum
        of Northern Arizona Ceramic
        Series, No. 3b. Flagstaff.

ADAMS, WILLIAM Y.

1959   Navajo and Anglo Reconstruc-
        tion of Prehistoric Sites in
        Southwestern Utah. American
        Antiquity, Vol. 25, No. 2,
        pp. 269-72. Washington, D.C.

1960   Ninety Years of Glen Canyon
        Archaeology, 1869-1959.
        Museum of Northern Arizona
        Bulletin, No. 33, Glen
        Canyon Series, No. 2.
        Flagstaff.

ADAMS, WILLIAM Y., and NETTIE K. ADAMS

1959   Inventory of Prehistoric
        Sites on the Lower San Juan
        River, Utah. Museum of Nor-
        thern Arizona Bulletin, No.
        31, Glen Canyon Series, No.
        1. Flagstaff.

ADAMS, WILLIAM Y., ALEXANDER J. LIND-
SAY and CHRISTY G. TURNER II

1958   Outline of Proposed Anthropo-
        logical Research in Glen Can-
        yon Basin. MS, Glen Canyon
        Office, Museum of Northern
        Arizona, Flagstaff. (Copy at
        National Park Service Head-
        quarters, Santa Fe, New
        Mexico.)

1961   Survey and Excavations in
        Lower Glen Canyon, 1952-1958.
        Museum of Northern Arizona
        Bulletin, No. 36, Glen Can-
        yon Series, No. 3. Flagstaff.

ADOVASIO, JAMES M.

1970a   The Origin, Development and
        Distribution of Western
        Archaic Textiles. Ph.D. dis-
        sertation, Department of
        Anthropology, University of
        Utah. Salt Lake City.

1970b   The Origin, Development and
        Distribution of Western Ar-
        chaic Textiles. Tebiwa, Vol.
        13, No. 2, pp. 1-40.
        Pocatello.

1970c Fremont Textiles. Paper pre-
       sented at the Fremont Culture
       Symposium, Society for Ameri-
       can Archaeology Meeting, May
       1970, Mexico City. MS, Depart-
       ment of Anthropology, Univer-
       sity of Utah. Salt Lake City.

1970d Chipped Stone Artifacts. In
       "Median Village and Fremont
       Culture Regional Variation,"
       John P. Marwitt. University
       of Utah Anthropological
       Papers, No. 95, pp. 75-87.
       Salt Lake City.

1974* Prehistoric North American
       Basketry. Nevada State
       Museum Anthropological
       Papers, No. 16. Carson City.

1975   Fremont Basketry. Tebiwa,
       Vol. 17, No. 2, pp. 67-73.
       Pocatello.

1976   Appendix I: Basketry from
       Swallow Shelter. In "Swallow
       Shelter and Associated Sites,"
       Gardiner F. Dalley, pp. 167-
       70. University of Utah
       Anthropological Papers, No.
       96. Salt Lake City.

ADOVASIO, JAMES M., and GARY F. FRY

1972   An Equilibrium Model for
       Culture Change in the Great
       Basin. In "Great Basin
       Cultural Ecology," Don D.
       Fowler (ed.). Desert Research
       Institute Publications in the
       Social Sciences, No. 8. Reno.

AGENBROAD, LARRY

1975* The Alluvian Geology of Up-
       per Grand Gulch, Utah: its
       Relationship to Anasazi In-
       habitation of the Cedar Mesa
       Area. In "Canyonlands Coun-
       try," Four Corners Geologi-
       cal Society Guidebook.

AIKENS, C. MELVIN

1961a A Sketch of Kayenta Anasazi,
       with a Comparative Trait List
       of Kayenta, Virgin Branch,
       Sevier-Fremont and Fremont
       Cultures. MS, Department of
       Anthropology, University of
       Utah. Salt Lake City.

1961b The Prehistory of Central and
       Northern Utah. Utah Archeo-
       logy, Vol. 7, No. 3, pp.
       3-15. Salt Lake City.

1962   The Archaeology of the
       Kaiparowits Plateau, South-
       eastern Utah. MA thesis,
       Department of Anthropology,
       University of Chicago. Chicago.

1963a Preliminary Report on Exca-
       vations in Southwestern Utah,
       1962. Utah Archeology, Vol.
       9, No. 1, pp. 6-10. Salt
       Lake City.

1963b Appendix II: Survey of Harris
       Wash. In "1961 Excavations,
       Harris Wash, Utah," Don D.
       Fowler. University of Utah
       Anthropological Papers, No.
       64, Glen Canyon Series, No.
       19, pp. 101-106. Salt Lake
       City.

1963c Appendix II: Kaiparowits
       Survey, 1961. In "1961
       Excavations, Kaiparowits
       Plateau, Utah," Don D. Fowler
       and C. Melvin Aikens. Uni-
       versity of Utah Anthropolo-
       gical Papers, No. 66, Glen
       Canyon Series, No. 20, pp.
       70-100. Salt Lake City.

1963d A Reappraisal of the Cultural
       Content and Relations of the
       Kayenta, Johnson, and Virgin
       Branch of the Southwestern
       Anasazi Culture. Ph.D. re-
       search proposal, Department
       of Anthropology, University
       of Utah. Salt Lake City.

1965a   Preliminary Report on Excavations at the Injun Creek Site, Warren, Utah. Utah Archeology, Vol. 11, No. 4, pp. 2-21. Salt Lake City.

1965b   Appendix I: Surveyed Sites in the Virgin Valley and Johnson Canyon. In "Excavations in Southwest Utah," C. Melvin Aikens. University of Utah Anthropological Papers, No. 76, Glen Canyon Series, No. 27, pp. 132-53. Salt Lake City.

1965c   Excavations in Southwest Utah. University of Utah Anthropological Papers, No. 76, Glen Canyon Series, No. 27. Salt Lake City.

1966a* Plains Relationships of the Fremont Culture: a Hypothesis Based on Excavations at Two Fremont-Promontory Sites in Northern Utah. Ph.D. dissertation, Department of Anthropology, University of Chicago. Chicago.

1966b   Plains Relationships of the Fremont Culture. Utah Archeology, Vol. 12, No. 4, pp. 3-12. Salt Lake City.

1966c   Fremont-Promontory-Plains Relationships. University of Utah Anthropological Papers, No. 82. Salt Lake City.

1966d   Virgin-Kayenta Cultural Relationships. University of Utah Anthropological Papers, No. 79, Glen Canyon Series, No. 29. Salt Lake City.

1967a   Hogup Mountain Cave. MS, Department of Anthropology, University of Utah. Salt Lake City.

1967b   Plains Relationships of the Fremont Culture: a Hypothesis. American Antiquity, Vol. 32, pp. 198-209. Washington, D.C.

1967c   Excavations at Snake Rock Village and the Bear River No. 2 Site. University of Utah Anthropological Papers, No. 87. Salt Lake City.

1969   Towards the Recognition of Cultural Diversity in Basin-Plateau Prehistory. In "Cultural Relations Between the Plateau and Great Basin," E.H. Swanson, Jr. (ed.). Northwest Anthropological Research Notes, Vol. 4, pp. 67-74. Moscow, Idaho.

1970a   Hogup Cave. University of Utah Anthropological Papers, No. 93. Salt Lake City.

1970b* Whence and Whither the Fremont Culture: a Restatement of the Problem. Paper presented at the Fremont Culture Symposium, Society for American Archaeology Meeting, May 1970, Mexico City.

1972   Fremont Culture: Restatement of Some Problems. American Antiquity, Vol. 37, pp. 61-66. Washington, D.C.

1976   Cultural Hiatus in the Eastern Great Basin? American Antiquity, Vol. 41, No. 4, pp. 543-48. Washington, D.C.

n.d.   A Proposal for a Travelling Glen Canyon Archeological Exhibit. MS, Department of Anthropology, University of Utah. Salt Lake City.

AIKENS, C. MELVIN, KIMBALL T. HARPER and GARY F. FRY

1967   Hogup Mountain Cave: Interim Report. Utah Archeology, Vol. 13, No. 4, pp. 5-11. Salt Lake City.

ALBEE, BEVERLY

n.d. Plant Communities in the Area of Sudden Shelter. In "Sudden Shelter," Jesse D. Jennings, Alan R. Schroedl, and Richard N. Holmer. University of Utah Anthropological Papers, in press. Salt Lake City.

ALEXANDER, WAYNE, and JAY W. RUBY

1963* 1962 Excavations at Summit, Utah: a Progress Report. Nevada State Museum Anthropological Papers, No. 9, pp. 17-32. Carson City.

ALTER, J. CECIL

1920 Some Cliff Dwellers of Today. Improvement Era, Vol. 24, No. 1, pp. 30-33. Salt Lake City.

1921 Utah's Cliff-dwelling Scenics. Improvement Era, Vol. 24, No. 4, pp. 301-306. Salt Lake City.

1928 Some Useful Early Indian References. Utah Historical Quarterly, Vol. 1, No. 1, pp. 26-32. Salt Lake City.

AMBLER, J. RICHARD

1959 A Preliminary Note on 1959 Excavations at the Coombs Site, Boulder, Utah. Utah Archeology, Vol. 5, No. 3, pp. 4-11. Salt Lake City.

1966a* Caldwell Village and Fremont Prehistory. Ph.D. dissertation, Department of Anthropology, University of Colorado. Boulder.

1966b Caldwell Village. University of Utah Anthropological Papers, No. 84. Salt Lake City.

1969 The Temporal Span of the Fremont. Southwestern Lore, Vol. 34, No. 4, pp. 107-117. Boulder.

1970* Just What is Fremont? Paper presented at the Fremont Culture Symposium, Society for American Archaeology Meeting, May 1970, Mexico City.

AMBLER, J. RICHARD, ALEXANDER J. LINDSAY, and MARY ANNE STEIN

1964 Survey and Excavations on Cummings Mesa, Arizona and Utah, 1960-1961. Museum of Northern Arizona Bulletin, No. 39, Glen Canyon Series, No. 5. Flagstaff.

AMSDEN, CHARLES AVERY

1949 Prehistoric Southwesterners from Basketmaker to Pueblo. Southwest Museum, Los Angeles.

ANDERSON, ADRIENNE

1975* Cultural Resource Assessment, Pilot Fire-flood Project, Glen Canyon NRA. Report, Midwest Archeological Center. Lincoln.

1976* Canyonlands National Park Resources Basic Inventory Program and Colorado River Trip, Trip Report. Report, Midwest Archeological Center. Lincoln.

ANDERSON, DUANE C.

1967 Stone Balls of the Fremont Culture: an Interpretation. Southwestern Lore, Vol. 32, No. 4, pp. 79-81. Boulder.

ANDERSON, EDGAR

1948 Appendix I: Racial Identity of the Corn from Castle Park. In "The Archaeology of

Castle Park Dinosaur National Monument," Robert Burgh and Charles Scoggin. University of Colorado Studies, Series in Anthropology, No. 2, pp. 91-92. Boulder.

1959　Zapalote Chico: an Important Chapter in the History of Maize and Man. Actas del 33 Congreso Internacional de Americanistas, pp. 230-37. San Jose, Costa Rica.

ANDERSON, KATHRYN

1964　Dripping Rocks Cave Site. Southwestern Lore, Vol. 30, No. 2, pp. 26-35. Boulder.

ANDERSON, KEITH M.

1960　Utah Virgin Branch Plain Utility Pottery. MA thesis, Department of Anthropology, University of Utah. Salt Lake City.

1961a　Archeological Survey of the El Paso Natural Gas Pipeline Right-of-Way from Thistle, Utah, to Las Vegas, Nevada. MS, Department of Anthropology, University of Utah. Salt Lake City.

1961b　Archeological Survey of Fish Spring National Wildlife Refuge. MS, Department of Anthropology, University of Utah. Salt Lake City.

1963　Ceramic Clues to Pueblo-Puebloid Relationships. American Antiquity, Vol. 28, No. 3, pp. 303-307. Washington, D.C.

ANDREWS, JANET

1971　The Cranial Morphology of the Prehistoric Great Basin Fremont Population. BA Honors thesis, Department of Anthropology, University of Utah. Salt Lake City.

1972　Paleopathology of the Eastern Great Basin Fremont Population. MA thesis, Department of Anthropology, University of Utah. Salt Lake City.

1977　Sevier Skeletal Material. In "Backhoe Village," David B. Madsen and La Mar W. Lindsay. Antiquities Section Selected Papers, Vol. 4, No. 12, pp. 93-103. Utah State Historical Society, Salt Lake City.

ANONYMOUS

1894a*　Review of "Catalogue of Cliff House and Cavern Relics," by Charles McLoyd and C.C. Graham. The Archaeologist, Vol. 2, p. 184. Waterloo.

1894b*　Mummies in the San Juan Valley. Newspaper article reprinted in The Archaeologist, Vol. 2, pp. 190-91. Waterloo.

1958　Flaming Gorge: Final Report, Preliminary Survey of the Flaming Gorge Reservoir, 1958. Report, Department of Anthropology, University of Utah. Salt Lake City.

1960　Ancient Indian Cultures. Allis-Chalmers Reporter, Jan.-Feb., pp. 11-15. Milwaukee.

ANTEVS, ERNST

1948　Climatic Changes and Pre-White Man. In "The Great Basin with Emphasis on Glacial and Postglacial Times." University of Utah Bulletin, Vol. 38, No. 20, Biological Series, Vol. 10, No. 7, pp. 168-91. Salt Lake City.

1950　Postglacial Climatic History of the Great Plains and Dating the Records of Man. In "Proceedings of the Sixth Plains Archeological Conference, 1948," Jesse D. Jennings (ed.). <u>University of Utah Anthropological Papers</u>, No. 11, pp. 46-50. Salt Lake City.

1953a   Geochronology of the Deglacial and Neothermal Ages. <u>The Journal of Geology</u>, Vol. 61, No. 3, pp. 195-230. Chicago.

1953b* The Postpluvial or Neothermal. <u>University of California Archaeological Survey Reports</u>, No. 22, pp. 9-23. Berkeley.

1955a* Geologic-Climatic Method of Dating. <u>In</u> "Geochronology," Terah L. Smiley (ed.). <u>University of Arizona Physical Science Bulletin</u>, No. 2, pp. 151-69. Tucson.

1955b   Geologic-Climatic Dating in the West. <u>American Antiquity</u>, Vol. 20, No. 4, pp. 317-35. Washington, D.C.

ARMELAGO, GEORGE J.

1968   Aikens' Fremont Hypothesis and Use of Skeletal Material in Archaeological Interpretation. <u>American Antiquity</u>, Vol. 33, No. 3, pp. 385-86. Washington, D.C.

ASCHMANN, HOMER H.

1958   Great Basin Climates in Relation to Human Occupance. <u>In</u> "Current Views on Great Basin Archaeology." <u>University of California Archaeological Survey Reports</u>, No. 42, pp. 23-40. Berkeley.

AUERBACH, H.S.

1943   Father Escalante's Journal, 1776-77; Newly Translated With Related Documents and Original Maps. <u>Utah Historical Quarterly</u>, Vol. 11. Salt Lake City.

AVERITT, BEEJ, and PAUL AVERITT

1947   Mastedon of Moab. <u>The Desert Magazine</u>, Vol. 10, No. 10, pp. 24-26. El Centro.

BALDWIN, GORDON C.

1946*   <u>Archaeological Survey: Beef Basin-Dark Canyon Plateau Areas of Southeastern Utah.</u> Report, Midwest Archeological Center. Lincoln.

1947   An Archaeological Reconnaissance of the Yampa and Green Rivers. <u>The Kiva</u>, Vol. 12, pp. 31-36. Tucson.

1949   Archaeological Survey in Southeastern Utah. <u>Southwestern Journal of Anthropology</u>, Vol. 5, No. 4, pp. 393-404. Albuquerque.

1950   The Pottery of the Southern Paiute. <u>American Antiquity</u>, Vol. 16, No. 1, pp. 50-56. Washington, D.C.

BANDELIER, ADOLPH F.

1890-   <u>Final Report of Investiga-</u>
1892   <u>tions Among the Indians of the Southwestern United States.</u> 2 vols. Cambridge.

BANNISTER, BRYANT

1964   Addendum: Beef Basin, Utah, Tree-Ring Materials. <u>In</u> "1962 Excavations, Glen Canyon Area," Floyd W. Sharrock, et al. <u>University of Utah Anthropological Papers</u>, No. 73, <u>Glen Canyon Series</u>, No. 25, pp. 173-75. Salt Lake City.

BANNISTER, BRYANT, J.S. DEAN, and W.J. ROBINSON

1969   <u>Tree-Ring Dates from Utah S-W: Southern Utah Area.</u> University of Arizona Laboratory of Tree-Ring Research, Tucson.

BARBER, EDWIN A.

1876a Ancient Pottery of Colorado,
Utah, Arizona and New Mexico.
American Naturalist, Vol. 10,
pp. 449-64. Boston.

1876b Rock Inscriptions of the
"Ancient Pueblos" of Colorado,
Utah, New Mexico and Arizona.
American Naturalist, Vol. 10,
pp. 716-25. Boston.

1877 Stone Implements and Orna-
ments from the Ruins of
Colorado, Utah, and Arizona.
American Naturalist, Vol. 11,
pp. 264-75. Boston.

BARTLETT, KATHARINE

n.d.* A Study of Human Skeletal
Material from Zion National
Park, Utah. Report, Midwest
Archeological Center. Lincoln.

BECHTEL CORPORATION

1973 Kaiparowits Project Environmental Report. MS, Department
of Anthropology, University
of Utah. Salt Lake City.

BECKWITH, E.G.

1855* Report of the Exploration for
a Route for the Pacific Rail-
road by Captain J.W. Gunnison,
Topographical Engineer, near
the 38th and 39th Parallels
of North Latitude. Reports
of Explorations and Surveys,
Vol. 2. Smithsonian Institution, Washington, D.C.

BECKWITH, FRANK

1927a To the Ancient Indian Hiero-
glyphics. Improvement Era,
Vol. 30, No. 4, pp. 343-45.
Salt Lake City.

1927b Rare Indian Curios. Improvement Era, Vol. 30, No. 5,
pp. 413-17. Salt Lake City.

1927c The Persistency of a Reli-
gious Ceremonial. Improvement Era, Vol. 30, No. 9,
pp. 785-94. Salt Lake City.

1927d The High Priest's Vestments.
Improvement Era, Vol. 30,
No. 11, pp. 1028-37.
Salt Lake City.

1931* Some Interesting Pictographs
in Nine Mile Canyon, Utah.
El Palacio, Vol. 31, No. 14,
pp. 216-22. Santa Fe.

1932 Serpent Petroglyph in Nine
Mile Canyon. El Palacio,
Vol. 33, Nos. 15-16, pp.
147-49. Santa Fe.

1934 Group of Petroglyphs near
Moab, Utah. El Palacio,
Vol. 36, Nos. 23-24, pp.
177-78. Santa Fe.

1935 Ancient Indian Petroglyphs
of Utah. El Palacio, Vol.
38, Nos. 6-8. pp. 33-40.
Santa Fe.

1940* Glyphs that Tell the Story
of an Ancient Migration.
Desert Magazine, Vol. 3,
No. 10, pp. 4-7. El Centro.

BEELEY, STEPHEN

1946 The Archeology of a Utah
Lake Site. MA thesis,
University of Utah Library.
Salt Lake City.

BENNETT, M. ANN

1975* Report of Archeological Clear-
ance Study: Utah Power and
Light Company Project,
Camp Williams -- Sigurd
Transmission Line.
World-Wide Survey Ltd.
Salt Lake City.

BENNYHOFF, J.A.

1958 The Desert West: a Trial
Correlation of Culture and
Chronology. University of

California Archaeological
Survey Reports, Vol. 42,
pp. 98-112. Berkeley.

BERGE, DALE L.

1964 An Archaeological Survey of
White Valley, Millard County,
Western Utah. MA thesis,
Department of Anthropology,
Brigham Young University.
Provo.

1973* An Archaeological Survey in
the Castle Valley Area,
Central Utah. MS, Department
of Anthropology, Brigham
Young University. Provo.

1974* An Archaeological Survey in
the Castle Valley Area,
Central Utah. _Publications
in Archaeology, New Series_,
No. 1. Brigham Young Uni-
versity Press, Provo.

1975* Archaeological Survey of the
Pinto-Abajo Transmission
Line, Southeastern Utah.
A Special Report. Brigham
Young University, Provo.

1976a* Cultural Resource Evaluation
of the Clear Creek Substation
-- Helper -- Blackhawk 46
K.V. Transmission Line,
Swisher Mine. Report to Utah
Power and Light Company. MS,
Department of Anthropology,
Brigham Young University.
Provo.

1976b* Archaeological Investigations
near Hanksville, Utah. Report
to Central Explorations Co.,
Inc., Oklahoma City. MS,
Department of Anthropology,
Brigham Young University.
Provo.

1977a* Cultural Resource Evaluation
near Cisco, Grand County,
Utah. Report to the Anachutz
Corporation. MS, Department of
Anthropology, Brigham Young
University. Provo.

1977b* Cultural Resource Evaluation
of the Trail Mountain Coal
Company Transmission Line.
Report to Utah Power and
Light Company. MS, Department
of Anthropology, Brigham
Young University. Provo.

1977c* Pictograph Site Evaluation
near Wellington, Carbon
County, Utah. Report to the
Pacific Gas and Electric
Company. MS, Department of
Anthropology, Brigham Young
University. Provo.

1977d* Cultural Resource Evaluation
of the Emery Substation --
Dog Valley Mine Distribution
Line. Report to Utah Power
and Light Company. MS,
Department of Anthropology,
Brigham Young University.
Provo.

BERGE, DALE L., and MICHAEL P. BENSON

1977* A Cultural Resource Evalua-
tion of the Emery Plant to
Emery City Transmission Line.
Report to Utah Power and
Light Company. MS, Department
of Anthropology, Brigham
Young University. Provo.

BERNHEIMER, CHARLES L.

1923 Encircling Navajo Mountain
with a Pack Train. _National
Geographic_, Vol. 43, No. 2,
pp. 197-224. Washington, D.C.

1929a Rainbow Bridge. Doubleday,
Doran and Company, New York.

1929b* Diary of the 1929 Bernheimer
Expedition. MS, Department of
Archaeology, American Museum
of Natural History. New York.
(Photocopy at Museum of Nor-
thern Arizona. Flagstaff.)

n.d.* Field Notes, Bernheimer Expeditions of 1922, 1923, 1924,
1926, 1927, 1929, 1930, for
the American Museum of Natur-

al History. MS, Utah State Historical Society. Salt Lake City.

BERRY, CLAUDIA HELM (see also, HELM, CLAUDIA F.)

1974   An Archeological Survey in Sevier, Emery and Garfield Counties. Utah Archeology, Vol. 20, No. 4, pp. 1-7. Salt Lake City.

n.d.*   Archeological Site West of Dinosaur National Monument, Utah. Report, Midwest Archeological Center. Lincoln.

BERRY, MICHAEL S.

1972a   Excavations at Evans Mound, 1970-71: an Interim Report. MS, Department of Anthropology, University of Utah. Salt Lake City.

1972b   The Evans Site. A Special Report. Department of Anthropology, University of Utah. Salt Lake City.

1974   The Evans Mound: Cultural Adaptation in Southwestern Utah. MA thesis, Department of Anthropology, University of Utah. Salt Lake City.

1975a   An Archeological Survey of the Northeast Portion of Arches National Park. Antiquities Section Selected Papers, Vol. 1, No. 3. Utah State Historical Society, Salt Lake City.

1975b   Archeological, Historical and Paleontological Survey for Consolidation Coal Company and Kemmerer Coal Company in Emery County, Utah. A Special Report. Antiquities Section, Utah State Historical Society. Salt Lake City.

1976a   Remnant Cave. In "Swallow Shelter and Associated Sites," Gardiner F. Dalley. University of Utah Anthropological Papers, No. 96, pp. 115-28. Salt Lake City.

1976b   No Name Valley. In "Swallow Shelter and Associated Sites," Gardiner F. Dalley. University of Utah Anthropological Papers, No. 96, pp. 145-61. Salt Lake City.

BERRY, MICHAEL S., and CLAUDIA F. BERRY

1976   An Archeological Reconnaissance of the White River Area, Northeastern Utah. Antiquities Section Selected Papers, Vol. 2, No. 4. Utah State Historical Society, Salt Lake City.

BIRNEY, HOFFMAN

1933*   Archaeological Sites in Glen Canyon of the Colorado: a Preliminary Report. MS, Peabody Museum, Harvard University. Cambridge.

BLACKWELDER, ELIOT

1939   Pleistocene Mammoths in Utah and Vicinity. American Journal of Science, Vol. 237, pp. 890-94. New Haven.

BLAIR, WILLIAM C.

1949   Additional Data on Crania from the Warren Mounds, Utah. American Antiquity, Vol. 14, No. 3, pp. 224-25. Washington, D.C.

BLAIR, WILLIAM C., and WALTER D. ENGER, JR.

1947   Crania from the Warren Mounds and their Possible Significance to Northern Periphery Archaeology. American Antiquity, Vol. 13, No. 2, pp. 142-46. Washington, D.C.

BOLTON, HERBERT E.

1950   <u>Pageant in the Wilderness:</u>
<u>the Story of the Escalante</u>
<u>Expedition to the Interior</u>
<u>Basin, 1776</u>. Utah State His-
torical Society, Salt Lake
City.

BOTELHO, EUGENE

1955   Pinto Basin Points in Utah.
<u>American Antiquity</u>, Vol. 21,
No. 2, pp. 185-86.
Washington, D.C.

BRANDLEY, ELSIE T.

1931   Cliffs and Caves of Southern
Utah. <u>Improvement Era</u>, Vol.
34, No. 5, pp. 268-70.
Salt Lake City.

BRETERNITZ, DAVID A.

1965*   <u>Archeological Survey in</u>
<u>Dinosaur National Monument,</u>
<u>Colorado-Utah, 1963-1964.</u>
Report, Midwest Archeological
Center. Lincoln.

1966   An Appraisal of Tree-Ring
Dated Pottery in the Southwest. <u>University of Arizona</u>
<u>Anthropological Papers</u>, No.
10. Tucson.

1970a   Archaeological Excavations in
Dinosaur National Monument,
Colorado-Utah, 1964-1965.
<u>University of Colorado</u>
<u>Studies</u>, <u>Series in Anthro-</u>
<u>pology</u>, No. 17. Boulder.

1970b* <u>The Eastern Uinta Fremont</u>.
Paper presented at the Fre-
mont Culture Symposium,
Society for American Archaeo-
logy Meeting, May 1970,
Mexico City.

BRETERNITZ, DAVID A., ARTHUR H. ROHN,
JR. and ELIZABETH A. MORRIS

1974*   Prehistoric Ceramics of the
Mesa Verde Region. <u>Museum of</u>
<u>Northern Arizona Ceramic</u>
<u>Series</u>, No. 5. Flagstaff.

BREW, JOHN O.

1946   Archaeology of Alkali Ridge,
Southeastern Utah, with a
Review of the Prehistory of
the Mesa Verde Division of
the San Juan and Some Observations on Archaeological
Systematics. <u>Peabody Museum</u>
<u>of American Archaeology and</u>
<u>Ethnology, Harvard University,</u>
<u>Papers</u>, Vol. 21. Cambridge.

BROOKS, RICHARD H., DANIEL O. LARSON
and MICHAEL COMPTON

1974*   <u>An Archaeological Report on</u>
<u>a Preliminary Reconnaissance</u>
<u>of the Proposed Eldorado/Kai-</u>
<u>parowits Transmission Line</u>
<u>Right-of-Way Corridor</u>. Report,
Nevada Archaeological Survey,
University of Nevada. Las
Vegas.

BROWN, F. MARTIN

1937   The Prehistoric Ruins of
Castle Park. <u>Southwestern</u>
<u>Lore</u>, Vol. 3, No. 2, pp.
22-28. Boulder.

n.d.*   The Yampa Canyon, Dinosaur
National Monument, Colorado-
Utah. MS, Midwest Archeologi-
cal Center. Lincoln.

BUCKLES, WILLIAM GAYL

1965   An Appraisal of Fremont Cul-
ture--Shoshonean Relationships. <u>Plains Anthropologist</u>,
Vol. 10, No. 27, pp. 54-55.
Lincoln.

BUETTNER-JANUSCH, JOHN

1954 Human Skeletal Material from Deadman Cave, Utah. University of Utah Anthropological Papers, No. 19. Salt Lake City.

BURGH, ROBERT F.

1950* A Fremont Basket Maker House in Dinsaur National Monument. Tree-Ring Bulletin, Vol. 16, No. 3, pp. 19-20. University of Arizona Laboratory of Tree-Ring Research, Tucson.

BURGH, ROBERT F., and CHARLES R. SCOGGIN

1948 The Archaeology of Castle Park, Dinosaur National Monument. University of Colorado Studies, Series in Anthropology, No. 2. Boulder.

BYE, R.A., JR.

1972 Ethnobotany of the Southern Paiute Indians in the 1870's; with a Note on the Early Ethnobotanical Contributions of Dr. Edward Palmer. In "Great Basin Cultural Ecology," Don D. Fowler (ed.). Desert Research Institute Publications in the Social Sciences, No. 8. Reno.

CALDWELL, DEAN

1974 The Lakeman Point. Utah Archeology, Vol. 20, No. 3, pp. 5-7. Salt Lake City.

1975 Utah Museum of Natural History Uncovers Mammoth Remains in Sandy, Utah. Utah Archeology, Vol. 21, No. 1, p. 6. Salt Lake City.

CALLEN, E.O., and PAUL S. MARTIN

1969 Plant Remains in Some Coprolites from Utah. American Antiquity, Vol. 34, No. 3, pp. 329-31. Washington, D.C.

CAMILLI, EILEEN

1975* Prehistoric Settlement Pattern on Cedar Mesa, Southeastern Utah. MA thesis, Northern Arizona University. Flagstaff.

CHAMBERLIN, RALPH V.

1908 Animal Names and Anatomical Terms of the Goshute Indians. Academy of Natural Science Proceedings, Vol. 9, pp. 74-103. Philadelphia. Also, Contributions from the Zoological Laboratory of Brigham Young University, No. 1, pp. 74-103. Provo.

1911 The Ethnobotany of the Gosiute Indians. Academy of Natural Science Proceedings, Vol. 63, pp. 24-99. Philadelphia. Also, American Anthropological Association Memoirs, Vol. 2, Pt. 5, pp. 329-405. Washington, D.C.

1913* Place and Personal Names of the Gosiute Indians of Utah. American Philosophical Society Proceedings, Vol. 52, No. 208. Philadelphia.

CHRISTENSEN, ROSS T.

1947* A Preliminary Report of Archaeological Investigations Near Utah Lake, Utah, 1946. MA thesis, Brigham Young University Library. Provo.

1949 On the Prehistory of Utah Valley. Utah Academy of Science, Arts, and Letters Proceedings, Vol. 25, pp. 101-111. Salt Lake City.

CLAFLIN, W.H.

n.d.* An Archaeological Reconnaissance into Southern Utah.

MS, Peabody Museum, Harvard
University. Cambridge.

CLARK, J. DESMOND

1964   Notes on Industries from Pine
         Springs (48Sw101) and Other
         Sites from Southern Wyoming.
         MS, Department of Anthropology,
         University of Utah. Salt Lake
         City.

CLARK, LEALAND L.

1975a   A 40,000-Year-Old Stone In-
         dustry on Lake Bonneville's
         Alpine Beach. Utah Archeology,
         Vol. 21, No. 1, pp. 1-5.
         Salt Lake City.

1975b   The Morphology of Stone Tools
         on Lake Bonneville's 40,000-
         Year-Old Alpine Beach. Utah
         Archeology, Vol. 21, No. 1,
         pp. 6-8. Salt Lake City.

CLARK, SUSAN R.

1966   Addendum: Tabular Summary of
         Plant and Animal Resources of
         the Glen Canyon. In "Corn,
         Cucurbits and Cotton from
         Glen Canyon," Hugh C. Cutler.
         University of Utah Anthro-
         pological Papers, No. 80,
         Glen Canyon Series, No. 30,
         p. 63. Salt Lake City.

CLEWLOW, C. WILLIAM, JR.

1967   Time and Space Relations of
         Some Great Basin Projectile
         Point Types. University of
         California Archaeology Sur-
         vey Reports, No. 70, pp.
         141-49. Berkeley.

COLTON, HAROLD S.

1952   Pottery Types of the Arizona
         Strip and Adjacent Areas in
         Utah and Nevada. Museum of
         Northern Arizona Ceramic
         Series, No. 1. Flagstaff.

1953   Potsherds; an Introduction to
         the Study of Prehistoric
         Southwestern Ceramics and
         Their Use in Historic Recon-
         struction. Museum of Northern
         Arizona Bulletin, No. 25.
         Flagstaff.

1955a   Pottery Types of the South-
         west. Museum of Northern Ari-
         zona Ceramic Series, No. 3a.
         Flagstaff.

1955b   Pottery Types of the South-
         west, Wares 8A, 8B, 9A, 9B,
         Tusayan Gray and White Ware,
         Little Colorado Gray and White
         Ware. Museum of Northern Ari-
         zona Ceramic Series, No. 3a.
         Flagstaff.

1955c   Checklist of Southwestern
         Pottery Types. Museum of
         Northern Arizona Ceramic
         Series, No. 2. Flagstaff.

1956   Pottery Types of the South-
         west, Wares 5A, 5B, 6B, 7A,
         7B, 7C, San Juan Red Ware,
         Tsegi Orange Ware, Homolovi
         Orange Ware, Winslow Orange
         Ware, Awatovi Yellow Ware,
         Jeddito Yellow Ware, Sicho-
         movi Red Ware. Museum of Nor-
         thern Arizona Ceramic Series,
         No. 3c. Flagstaff.

1962   Steamboating in the Glen
         Canyon of the Colorado River.
         Plateau, Vol. 35, No. 2, pp.
         57-59. Flagstaff.

COLTON, HAROLD S., and LYNDON L. HAR-
GRAVE

1937   Handbook of Northern Arizona
         Pottery Wares. Museum of Nor-
         thern Arizona Bulletin, No.
         11. Flagstaff.

CONDIE, KENT C., and A. BLAXLAND

1970   Appendix IX: Sources of Obsi-
         dian in Hogup and Danger
         Caves. In "Hogup Cave," C.
         Melvin Aikens. University of

Utah Anthropological Papers, No. 93. Salt Lake City.

COOLEY, MAURICE E.

1958   Physiography of the Glen-San Juan Canyon Area, Part I. *Plateau*, Vol. 31, No. 2, pp. 21-33. Flagstaff.

1959a   Physiography of the Glen-San Juan Canyon Area, Part II: Physiography of San Juan Canyon. *Plateau*, Vol. 31, No. 3, pp. 49-56. Flagstaff.

1959b   Physiography of the Glen-San Juan Canyon Area, Part III: Physiography of Glen and Cataract Canyons. *Plateau*, Vol. 31, No. 4, pp. 73-79. Flagstaff.

COOLEY, MAURICE E., and W.F. HARDT

1961   Relation of Geology to Hydrology in the Segi Mesas Area, Utah and Arizona. *Arizona Geological Society Digest*, Vol. 4, pp. 59-68. Tucson.

1962   Late Pleistocene and Recent Erosion and Alluviation in Parts of the Colorado River System, Arizona and Utah. *U.S. Geological Survey Professional Papers*, No. 450-B, pp. 48-50. Washington, D.C.

COULAM, NANCY J., and PEGGY BARNETT

1976   Paleoethnobotanical Analysis. In "Sudden Shelter," Jesse D. Jennings, Alan R. Schroedl and Richard N. Holmer. *University of Utah Anthropological Papers*, in press. Salt Lake City.

CRAMPTON, C. GREGORY

1959   Outline History of the Glen Canyon Region, 1776-1922. *University of Utah Anthropological Papers*, No. 42, *Glen Canyon Series*, No. 9. Salt Lake City.

1960   Historical Sites in Glen Canyon, Mouth of San Juan River to Lees Ferry. *University of Utah Anthropological Papers*, No. 46, *Glen Canyon Series*, No. 12. Salt Lake City.

1962   Historical Sites in Glen Canyon, Mouth of Hansen Creek to Mouth of San Juan River. *University of Utah Anthropological Papers*, No. 61, *Glen Canyon Series*, No. 17. Salt Lake City.

1964a   San Juan Canyon Historical Sites. *University of Utah Anthropological Papers*, No. 70, *Glen Canyon Series*, No. 22. Salt Lake City.

1964b   Addendum of New Data Relating to Areas Covered in Previous Reports. In "Historical Sites in Cataract and Narrow Canyons and in Glen Canyon to California Bar," C. Gregory Crampton. *University of Utah Anthropological Papers*, No. 72, *Glen Canyon Series*, No. 24, pp. 65-72. Salt Lake City.

1964c   Historical Sites in Cataract and Narrow Canyons and in Glen Canyon to California Bar. *University of Utah Anthropological Papers*, No. 72, *Glen Canyon Series*, No. 24. Salt Lake City.

1964d   *Standing Up Country: the Canyon Lands of Utah and Arizona*. Alfred A. Knopf, New York. University of Utah Press, Salt Lake City, in association with the Amon Carter Museum of Western Art, Fort Worth.

CRAMPTON C. GREGORY, and DWIGHT L. SMITH (eds.)

1961   The Hoskaninni Papers, Mining in Glen Canyon, 1897-1902, by Robert B. Stanton. *University of Utah Anthropological Papers*, No. 54, *Glen Canyon Series*, No. 15. Salt Lake City.

CREER, LELAND H.

1958   The Activities of Jacob Hamblin in the Region of the Colorado. *University of Utah Anthropological Papers*, No. 33, *Glen Canyon Series*, No. 4, Salt Lake City.

CROSS, JOHN L.

1960   The Artifacts of Camp Maple Dell, Payson Canyon, Utah County, Utah. *Utah Archeology*, Vol. 6, No. 2, pp. 11-15. Salt Lake City.

1962   Report of an Indian Skull Find. *Utah Archeology*, Vol. 8, No. 1, pp. 14-16. Salt Lake City.

1963   Unusual Petroglyph Find in Utah (West Canyon, Utah County). *Utah Archeology*, Vol. 9, No. 1, p. 1. Salt Lake City.

CROUSE, HUBERT Y.

1954   A Folsom Point from the Uinta Basin, Utah. *The Masterkey*, Vol. 28, No. 1, pp. 50-51. Los Angeles.

CUMMINGS, BYRON

1910   The Ancient Inhabitants of the San Juan Valley. *University of Utah Bulletin*, Vol. 3, No. 3, Pt. II. Salt Lake City.

1915   The Kivas of the San Juan Drainage. *American Anthropologist*, Vol. 17, No. 2, pp. 272-282. Washington, D.C.

1930a* *Segazlin Mesa, Surface Pueblo Ruins*. Field Notes MS, Arizona Pioneers' Historical Society. Tucson.

1930b* *Byron Cummings Expedition: Navajo Mountain and Nitsin Canyon*. Unpublished journal of June 28-August 27, 1930, Arizona Pioneers' Historical Society. Tucson.

1934*   Letter to Lyndon L. Hargrave, dated March 6, 1934; quoted in Hargrave, 1935, pp. 12-14.

CURREY, DONALD R.

1976   Late Quaternary Geomorphic History of Ivie Creek and Sudden Shelter. *In* "Sudden Shelter," Jesse D. Jennings, Alan R. Schroedl and Richard N. Holmer. *University of Utah Anthropological Papers*, in press. Salt Lake City.

CUTLER, HUGH C.

1966a   Corn, Cucurbits and Cotton from Glen Canyon. *University of Utah Anthropological Papers*, No. 80, *Glen Canyon Series*, No. 30. Salt Lake City.

1966b   Appendix VI: Maize of Caldwell Village. *In* "Caldwell Village," J. Richard Ambler. *University of Utah Anthropological Papers*, No. 84, pp. 114-18. Salt Lake City.

1968   Appendix I: Plant Remains from Sites near Navajo Mountain. *In* "Survey and Excavations North and East of Navajo Mountain, Utah, 1959-1962," Alexander J. Lindsay, Jr., et al. *Museum of Northern Arizona Bulletin*, No. 45, *Glen Canyon Series*, No. 8, pp. 371-78. Flagstaff.

1970   Appendix VII: Corn from Hogup Cave, a Fremont Site. *In* "Hogup Cave," C. Melvin Aikens. *University of Utah Anthropological Papers*, No. 93, pp. 271-72. Salt Lake City.

CUTLER, HUGH C., and LEONARD BLAKE

1970   Appendix I: Corn from the Median Village Site. *In* "Median Village and Fremont Culture Regional Variation," John P. Marwitt. *University of*

Utah Anthropological Papers, No. 95. Salt Lake City.

CUTLER, HUGH C., and JOHN W. BOWER

1961   Appendix: Plant Materials from Several Glen Canyon Sites. In "Survey and Excavations in Lower Glen Canyon, 1952-1958," William Y. Adams, Alexander J. Lindsay, Jr., and Christy G. Turner II. Museum of Northern Arizona Bulletin, No. 36, Glen Canyon Series, No. 3, pp. 58-61. Flagstaff.

DALLEY, GARDINER F.

1970a   Artifacts of Wood. In "Hogup Cave," C. Melvin Aikens. University of Utah Anthropological Papers, No. 93, pp. 153-86. Salt Lake City.

1970b   Worked Bone and Antler. In "Median Village and Fremont Regional Variation," John P. Marwitt. University of Utah Anthropological Papers, No. 95, pp. 96-134. Salt Lake City.

1972a   Worked Stone. In "The Evans Site," Michael S. Berry. A Special Report, pp. 97-108. Department of Anthropology, University of Utah. Salt Lake City.

1972b   Worked Bone and Antler. In "The Evans Site," Michael S. Berry. A Special Report, pp. 119-43. Department of Anthropology, University of Utah. Salt Lake City.

1972c   Appendix I: Palynology of the Evans Mound Deposits. In "The Evans Site," Michael S. Berry. A Special Report, pp. 187-94. Department of Anthropology, University of Utah. Salt Lake City.

1972d   The Impact of Buried Cable Construction Activities on Archeological and Historic Resources in the Golden Spike NHS. Report, Midwest Archeological Center. Lincoln.

1972e   A Preliminary Report on Archeological Activities Accomplished Under the Provisions of United States Department of the Interior Antiquities Act Permits. Report, Midwest Archeological Center. Lincoln.

1973   Alternate Village. In "Highway U-95 Archeology: Comb Wash to Grand Flat," Gardiner F. Dalley (ed.). A Special Report, pp. 29-62. Department of Anthropology, University of Utah. Salt Lake City.

1976a   Appendix II: Palynology of the Swallow Shelter Deposits. In "Swallow Shelter and Associated Sites," Gardiner F. Dalley. University of Utah Anthropological Papers, No. 96. Salt Lake City.

1976b   Swallow Shelter and Associated Sites. University of Utah Anthropological Papers, No. 96. Salt Lake City.

n.d.   Rock Art of Utah. MS, Department of Anthropology, University of Utah. Salt Lake City.

(ED.)

1973   Highway U-95 Archeology: Comb Wash to Grand Flat. A Special Report. Department of Anthropology, University of Utah. Salt Lake City.

DANSON, EDWARD B.

1958   The Glen Canyon Project.
        Plateau, Vol. 30, No. 3,
        pp. 75-78. Flagstaff.

DAVIS, LARRY D.

1970*   A Study of the Distribution
        and Stylistic Variation of
        Figurines within the Fremont
        Culture Area. Paper presented
        at the Fremont Culture Sympo-
        sium Society for American
        Archaeology Meeting, May 1970,
        Mexico City.

1975*   An Archaeological Survey of
        North Cottonwood Canyon, San
        Juan County, Southeastern
        Utah. MA thesis, Department
        of Anthropology, Brigham
        Young University. Provo.

DAY, KENT C.

1961   Archeological Survey and
        Testing in Moqui Canyon and
        Castle Wash, 1961. Utah
        Archeology, Vol. 7, No. 4,
        pp. 12-14. Salt Lake City.

1963a   Preliminary Report of the
        Flaming Gorge Survey. Utah
        Archeology, Vol. 8, No. 4,
        pp. 3-7. Salt Lake City.

1963b   Appendix II: Moqui Canyon and
        Castle Wash Survey. In "1961
        Excavations, Glen Canyon
        Area," Floyd W. Sharrock,
        Kent C. Day and David S.
        Dibble. University of Utah
        Anthropological Papers, No.
        63, Glen Canyon Series, No.
        18, pp. 237-305. Salt Lake
        City.

1963c   Addendum II: Lithic Sites in
        Sanpete County, Utah. In
        "Archeological Survey of the
        Flaming Gorge Reservoir Area,
        Wyoming-Utah," Kent C. Day,
        and David S. Dibble. Univer-

sity of Utah Anthropological
Papers, No. 65, Upper Colorado
Series, No. 9. Salt Lake City.

1964a   Appendix II: Survey and Tested
        Sites. In "1962 Excavations,
        Glen Canyon Area," Floyd W.
        Sharrock, et al. University of
        Utah Anthropological Papers,
        No. 73, Glen Canyon Series,
        No. 25, pp. 139-56. Salt Lake
        City.

1965   Archeological Survey of the
        Uinta Basin, Northeastern Utah.
        Report prepared in connection
        with NSF Grant GS-652, Depart-
        ment of Anthropology, Univer-
        sity of Utah. Salt Lake City.

1966a   Preliminary Report on Excava-
        tions at Gunlock Flats,
        Southwestern Utah. Utah
        Archeology, Vol. 12, No. 2,
        pp. 2-9. Salt Lake City.

1966b   Excavations at Gunlock Flats,
        Southwestern Utah. University
        of Utah Anthropological
        Papers, No. 83, Miscellaneous
        Collected Papers, No. 11.
        Salt Lake City.

DAY, KENT C., and DAVID S. DIBBLE

1963   Archeological Survey of the
        Flaming Gorge Reservoir
        Area, Wyoming-Utah. Univer-
        sity of Utah Anthropological
        Papers, No. 65, Upper Colorado
        Series, No. 9. Salt Lake
        City.

DEAN, JEFFREY S.

1964   Summary of Tree-Ring Material
        from Southern Utah. In
        "1962 Excavations, Glen Can-
        yon Area," Floyd W. Sharrock,
        et al. University of Utah
        Anthropological Papers, No.
        73, Glen Canyon Series, No.
        25, pp. 167-73. Salt Lake
        City.

DEBLOOIS, EVAN

    1966   Archeological Studies in
Central Utah. MS, Department
of Anthropology, University
of Utah. Salt Lake City.

    1969   Some Historic Indian Burials
from Utah Valley. Utah Archeology, Vol. 15, No. 4, pp.
3-7. Salt Lake City.

DE HAAN, PETRUS A.

    1972*   An Archaeological Survey of
Lower Montezuma Canyon,
Southeastern Utah. MA thesis,
Department of Anthropology,
Brigham Young University.
Provo.

DESART, D.J.

    1970*   A Study of Paiute and Shoshone
Pottery. MS, Western Studies
Center, Desert Research Insti-
tute. Reno.

DELLENBAUGH, F.S.

    1877*   The Shinumos - a Pre-Historic
People of the Rocky Mountain
Region. Buffalo Society of
Natural Sciences Bulletin,
Vol. 3, No. 4.

    1926*   A Canyon Voyage: the Narrative
of the Second Powell Expedi-
tion Down the Green-Colorado
River from Wyoming and the
Explorations on Land in the
Years 1871 and 1872. 2nd
edition. New Haven.

DEROSS, ROSE M.

    1958   Adventures of Georgie White,
TV's "Woman of the Rivers."
Desert Magazine Press, Palm
Desert, California.

DIBBLE, CHARLES E.

    1940a   Some Stone Implements of the
Deep Creek Area of Utah.
Archeology and Ethnology Pa-
pers, No. 5. Museum of Anthro-
pology, University of Utah.
Salt Lake City. Also, in "The
Archeology of the Deep Creek
Region, Utah," C. Malouf, C.E.
Dibble and E. Smith. University
of Utah Anthropological Papers,
No. 5, pp. 65-70. Salt Lake
City.

    1940b* Recent Archaeological Investi-
gations of the Great Salt Lake
Region of Utah. Institute
Nacional de Anthropologia e
Historia, pp. 207-208. Mexi-
co City.

DIBBLE, DAVID S.

    1962a   Archeological Survey of the
Whitney Reservoir Area, Summit
County (42Sm00), Utah. MS,
Department of Anthropology,
University of Utah. Salt Lake
City.

    1962b   Preliminary Archeological
Survey of the Flaming Gorge
Reservoir, Utah-Wyoming. MS,
Department of Anthropology,
University of Utah. Salt
Lake City.

DIBBLE, DAVID S., and KENT C. DAY

    1962   A Preliminary Survey of the
Fontenelle Reservoir, Wyoming.
University of Utah Anthro-
pological Papers, No. 58,
Upper Colorado Series, No. 7.
Salt Lake City.

DICK, HERBERT W.

    1949*   Report on Archaeological
Research in the Yampa and
Green River Canyons, Dinosaur
National Monument, 1949. MS,
Dinosaur National Monument
Headquarters. Jensen.

1950* Report of Archaeological Research in the Yampa and Green River Canyons, Dinosaur National Monument and Adjacent Areas, 1950. MS, University of Colorado Museum. Boulder.

n.d.* The Archaeology of Marigold's Cave, Castle Park, Dinosaur National Monument. MS, University of Colorado Museum. Boulder.

DOUGLASS, WILLIAM B.

1908* Field Notes of the Survey of the Reservations Embracing the Natural Bridges National Monument, the Cigarette Cave and the Snow Flat Cave (or Prehistoric Cave Springs No. 1 and No. 2). MS, Natural Bridges National Monument.

DUFFIELD, M.S.

1904 Aboriginal Remains in Nevada and Utah. American Anthropologist, Vol. 6, pp. 148-50. Washington, D.C.

DURRANT, STEPHEN D.

1970 Appendix II: Faunal Remains as Indicators of Neothermal Climates at Hogup Cave. In "Hogup Cave," C. Melvin Aikens. University of Utah Anthropological Papers, No. 93, pp. 241-46. Salt Lake City.

DURRANT, STEPHEN D., and NOWLAN K. DEAN

1960 Mammals of Flaming Gorge Reservoir Basin. In "Ecological Studies of the Flora and Fauna of the Flaming Gorge Reservoir Basin, Utah and Wyoming," Seville Flowers, et al. University of Utah Anthropological Papers, No. 48, Upper Colorado Series, No. 3, pp. 209-235. Salt Lake City.

DURRANT, STEPHEN D., and SEVILLE FLOWERS

1962 A Survey of Vegetation in the Curecanti Reservoir Basins. University of Utah Anthropological Papers, No. 56, Upper Colorado Series, No. 6, Salt Lake City.

DYKMAN, JAMES L.

1976 High Altitude Anasazi Lithic Assemblage: 1972 Elk Ridge Archaeological Project, Manti LaSal National Forest, Monticello District, Southeastern Utah: Description, Classification, and Cultural Inference. MA thesis, Department of Anthropology, Brigham Young University. Provo.

DYKMAN, JAMES L., and RICHARD A. THOMPSON

1976* The Dog Valley Strip Mine Survey. A Special Report. Southern Utah State College. Cedar City.

EARLE, B.J.

1975* An Archaeological Summary of the Wasatch Plateau, Central Utah. MS, Museum of Archaeology and Ethnology, Brigham Young University. Provo.

ENGER, WALTER D.

1942 Archeology of Blackrock 3 Cave, Utah. Archeology and Ethnology Papers, Museum of Anthropology, University of Utah, No. 7. Also, University of Utah Anthropological Papers, No. 7 (1950). Salt Lake City.

ENGER, WALTER D., and WILLIAM C. BLAIR

 1947   Crania from the Warren Mounds
        and their Possible Signifi-
        cance to Northern Periphery
        Archaeology. American Anti-
        quity, Vol. 13, No. 2, pp.
        142-46. Washington, D.C.

EPSTEIN, J.F.

 1968* An Archeological View of Uto-
        Aztekan Time Perspective. In
        "Utaztekan Prehistory," E.H.
        Swanson, Jr. (ed.). Idaho
        State University Museum Occa-
        sional Papers, No. 22, pp.
        106-130. Pocatello.

ESCALANTE, SILVESTRE V.D.

 1943   Father Escalante's Journal,
        1776-77. Newly translated
        with related documents and
        original maps, by Herbert S.
        Auerbach. Utah Historical
        Quarterly, Vol. 11, Nos. 1-4.
        Salt Lake City.

EULER, ROBERT C.

 1964   Southern Paiute Archaeology.
        American Antiquity, Vol. 29,
        No. 3, pp. 379-81. Washing-
        ton, D.C.

 1966   Southern Paiute Ethnohistory.
        University of Utah Anthro-
        pological Papers, No. 78,
        Glen Canyon Series, No. 28.
        Salt Lake City.

EULER, ROBERT C., and HARRY L. NAYLOR

 1952* Southern Ute Rehabilitation
        Planning: a Study in Self
        Determination. Human Organi-
        zation, Vol. 11, pp. 27-32.
        Boulder.

FARMER, MALCOLM F.

 1952* A Brief Report on Archaeolo-
        gical Work on Lands Bordering
        the Navajo Indian Reservation,
        1950-1951. MS, Natural Bridges
        National Monument.

FERGUSON, C.W., JR.

 1949   Additional Dates for Nine
        Mile Canyon, Northeastern
        Utah. Tree-Ring Bulletin,
        Vol. 16, No. 2, pp. 10-11.
        Tucson.

FEWKES, J. WALTER

 1917* Prehistoric Remains in New
        Mexico, Colorado, and Utah.
        Smithsonian Miscellaneous
        Collections, Vol. 66, No. 17,
        pp. 76-92. Washington, D.C.

 1918a* Archaeological Investigations
        in New Mexico, Colorado, and
        Utah. Smithsonian Miscellan-
        eous Collections, Vol. 68,
        No. 1, pp. 1-38. Washington,
        D.C.

 1918b* Prehistoric Ruins in South-
        western Colorado and South-
        eastern Utah. Smithsonian
        Miscellaneous Collections,
        Vol. 68, No. 12, pp. 108-133.
        Washington, D.C.

 1919* Archaeological Field Work in
        Southwest Colorado and Utah
        in 1918. Smithsonian Miscel-
        laneous Collections, Vol. 70,
        No. 2. Washington, D.C.

 1923   The Hovenweep National Monu-
        ment. American Anthropolo-
        gist, n.s. Vol. 25, No. 2, pp.
        145-55. Washington, D.C.

FISH, PAUL R.

 1974* Archaeological and Ethnohis-
        torical Phase I Consultation
        for the Kaiparowits Power
        Project, Proposed Plant Sites,
        Impact Study Area, and Pro-
        posed Transmission Line Corri-
        dors: Preliminary Report.
        MS, Museum of Northern Arizo-
        na. Flagstaff.

FISHER, STANLEY A.

1953 In the Beginning: a Navaho Creation Myth. <u>University of Utah Anthropological Papers</u>, No. 13. Salt Lake City.

FLAIM, FRANCIS, and AUSTEN D. WARBURTON

1961 Additional Figurines from Rasmussen Cave. <u>The Masterkey</u>, Vol. 35, No. 1, pp. 19-24. Los Angeles.

FLOWERS, SEVILLE

1959a Vegetation of Glen Canyon. In "Ecological Studies of the Flora and Fauna in Glen Canyon," Angus M. Woodbury, et al. <u>University of Utah Anthropological Papers</u>, No. 40, <u>Glen Canyon Series</u>, No. 7, pp. 21-62. Salt Lake City.

1959b Appendix D: Algae Collected in Glen Canyon. In "Ecological Studies of the Flora and Fauna in Glen Canyon," Angus M. Woodbury, et al. <u>University of Utah Anthropological Papers</u>, No. 40, <u>Glen Canyon Series</u>, No. 7, pp. 203-206. Salt Lake City.

FLOWERS, SEVILLE, et al.

1960 Ecological Studies of the Flora and Fauna of the Flaming Gorge Reservoir Basin, Utah and Wyoming. <u>University of Utah Anthropological Papers</u>, No. 48, <u>Upper Colorado Series</u>, No. 3. Salt Lake City.

FONNER, R.L.

1957 Appendix B,b: Mammal Feces from Danger Cave. In "Danger Cave," Jesse D. Jennings. <u>University of Utah Anthropological Papers</u>, No. 27, p. 303. Salt Lake City.

FORSYTH, DONALD W.

1972 <u>A Preliminary Classification of Anasazi Ceramics from Montezuma Canyon, San Juan County, Southeastern Utah.</u> MS, Department of Anthropology, Brigham Young University. Provo.

FOSTER, GENE

1952 A Brief Archeological Survey of Glen Canyon. <u>Plateau</u>, Vol. 25, No. 2, pp. 21-26. Flagstaff.

1954 Petrographic Art in Glen Canyon. <u>Plateau</u>, Vol. 27, No. 1, pp. 6-18. Flagstaff.

FOWLER, CATHERINE SWEENEY

1966 Environmental Setting and Natural Resources. In "Southern Paiute Ethnohistory," Robert C. Euler. <u>University of Utah Anthropological Papers</u>, No. 78, pp. 13-31. Salt Lake City.

1969* Great Basin Anthropology -- a Bibliography. <u>Desert Research Institute Publications in the Social Sciences</u>, No. 5. Reno.

1972a* <u>Comparative Numic Ethnobiology</u>. Ph.D. dissertation, University of Pittsburgh. Pittsburgh.

1972b Some Ecological Clues to Proto-Numic Homelands. In "Great Basin Cultural Ecology," Don D. Fowler (ed.). <u>Desert Research Institute Publications in the Social Sciences</u>, No. 8, pp. 105-121. Reno.

FOWLER, DON D.

1958   Archeological Survey in Glen Canyon: a Preliminary Report of 1958 Work. Utah Archeology, Vol. 4, No. 4, pp. 14-16. Salt Lake City.

1959   Glen Canyon Main Stem Survey. In "The Glen Canyon Archeological Survey, Part II," Don D. Fowler, et al. University of Utah Anthropological Papers, No. 39, Glen Canyon Series, No. 6, pp. 473-540. Salt Lake City.

1960   Survey of Upper Moqui Canyon. MS, Department of Anthropology, University of Utah. Salt Lake City.

1961a   Appendix II: Lake Canyon Survey. In "1960 Excavations, Glen Canyon Area," Floyd W. Sharrock, et al. University of Utah Anthropological Papers, No. 52, Glen Canyon Series, No. 14. Salt Lake City.

1961b   1960 Archeological Survey and Testing in the Glen Canyon Region. Utah Archeology, Vol. 7, No. 1, pp. 18-24. Salt Lake City.

1963   1961 Excavations, Harris Wash, Utah. University of Utah Anthropological Papers, No. 64, Glen Canyon Series, No. 19. Salt Lake City.

1970   The Western Fremont. Paper presented at the Fremont Culture Symposium, Society for American Archaeology Meeting, May 1970, Mexico City. MS, Department of Anthropology, University of Utah. Salt Lake City.

(ED.)

1972   Great Basin Cultural Ecology. Desert Research Institute Publications in the Social Sciences, No. 8. Reno.

FOWLER, DON D., and C. MELVIN AIKENS

1962   A Preliminary Report of 1961 Excavations in Harris Wash and on the Kaiparowits Plateau. Utah Archeology, Vol. 8, No. 1, pp. 5-13. Salt Lake City.

1963   1961 Excavation, Kaiparowits Plateau, Utah. University of Utah Anthropological Papers, No. 66, Glen Canyon Series, No. 20. Salt Lake City.

FOWLER, DON D., and DAVID B. MADSEN

n.d.*   Southeastern Great Basin Archaeology. In Great Basin volume, W.L.d'Azevedo (ed.). Smithsonian Institution Handbook of North American Indians, in press. Washington, D.C.

FOWLER, DON D., DAVID B. MADSEN and E.M. HATTORI

1973*   Prehistory of Southeastern Nevada. Desert Research Institute Publications in the Social Sciences, No. 6. Reno.

FOWLER, DON D., and JOHN F. MATLEY

1978   The Palmer Collection from Southwestern Utah, 1875. University of Utah Anthropological Papers, No. 99, Miscellaneous Collected Papers, No. 20, in press. Salt Lake City.

1979*   The Material Culture of the Numa: the John Wesley Powell Collection from the Great Basin, 1868-1877. Smithsonian Contributions to Anthropology, in press. Washington, D.C.

FOWLER, DON D., et al.

1959   The Glen Canyon Archeological Survey, Parts I, II, and III. University of Utah Anthropological Papers, No. 39, Glen Canyon Series, No. 6. Salt Lake City.

FRY, GARY F.

1968   Prehistoric Diet at Danger Cave, Utah: as Determined by the Analysis of Coprolites. MA thesis, Department of Anthropology, University of Utah. Salt Lake City.

1970a   Prehistoric Human Ecology in Utah: Based on the Analysis of Coprolites. Ph.D. dissertation, Department of Anthropology, University of Utah. Salt Lake City.

1970b   Salt Lake Fremont. Paper presented at the Fremont Culture Symposium, Society for American Archaeology Meeting, May 1970, Mexico City. MS, Department of Anthropology, University of Utah. Salt Lake City.

1970c   Appendix III: Preliminary Analysis of Hogup Cave Coprolites. In "Hogup Cave," C. Melvin Aikens. University of Utah Anthropological Papers, No. 93, pp. 247-50. Salt Lake City.

1972*   Prehistoric Territoriality: a Case Study from the Eastern Great Basin. Paper presented at the Great Basin Anthropological Conference, Salt Lake City.

FRY, GARY F., and JAMES M. ADOVASIO

1970   Population Differentiation in Hogup and Danger Caves, Two Archaic Sites in the Eastern Great Basin. In "Five Papers on the Archaeology of the Desert West," D.R. Tuohy, D.L.

Kendall and P.A. Crowell (eds.) Nevada State Museum Anthropological Papers, No. 15, pp. 208-215. Carson City.

FRY, GARY F., and GARDINER F. DALLEY

n.d.   The Levee and Knoll Sites. University of Utah Anthropological Papers, in press. Salt Lake City.

FRY, GARY F., and HENRY J. HALL

1969   Parasitological Examination of Prehistoric Human Coprolites from Utah. Utah Academy of Science, Arts and Letters Proceedings. Salt Lake City.

FRY, GARY F., and JOHN G. MOORE

1969   Enterobius vermicularis: 10000 Year Old Human Infection. Science, Vol. 166, p. 1620. Washington, D.C.

GAEDE, MARC, and MARNIE GAEDE

1977*   100 Years of Erosion at Poncho House. The Kiva, Vol. 43, No. 1, pp. 37-48. Tucson.

GALINAT, WALTON C., and JAMES H. GUNNERSON

1969   Fremont Maize. In "The Fremont Culture: a Study in Culture Dynamics of the Northern Anasazi Frontier," James H. Gunnerson. Peabody Museum of American Archaeology and Ethnology, Harvard University, Papers, Vol. 59, No. 2, pp. 198-206. Cambridge.

GAUMER, ALFRED E.

1937*   Basketmaker Caves in Desolation Canyon, Green River, Utah. The Masterkey, Vol. 11, No. 5, pp. 160-65. Los Angeles.

1939*   A Fremont River Culture Cradle. The Masterkey, Vol. 13, No. 4, pp. 139-40. Los Angeles.

GILLIN, JOHN P.

1936 Excavations at Nephi. MS, Department of Anthropology, University of Utah. Salt Lake City.

1938 Archeological Investigations in Nine Mile Canyon, Utah. University of Utah Bulletin, Vol. 28, No. 11. Also, University of Utah Anthropological Papers, No. 21 (1955). Salt Lake City.

1941 Archaeological Investigations in Central Utah. Peabody Museum of American Archaeology and Ethnology, Harvard University, Papers, Vol. 17, No. 2. Cambridge.

GILLIO, DAVID A.

1975a* Archeological Survey of Crandall Canyon Mine Road. Report, U.S. Forest Service. Richfield.

1975b* Archeological Survey of North Dragon Limestone Mine. Report, U.S. Forest Service. Richfield.

1975c* Archeological Survey of Lowry Water Bridge Site. Report, U.S. Forest Service. Richfield.

1975d* Archeological Survey of Trail Mountain Timber Sale. Report, U.S. Forest Service. Richfield.

1975e* Revised Archeological Estimate for Paradise Valley Area. Report, U.S. Forest Service, Intermountain Region. Ogden.

GILSEN, LELAND

1968* An Archaeological Survey of Goshen Valley, Utah County, Central Utah. MA thesis, Department of Anthropology, Brigham Young University. Provo.

GOSS, JAMES A.

1964 Cultural Development in the Great Basin. Utah Archeology, Vol. 10, No. 2, pp. 8-13; No. 3, pp. 4-13; No. 4, pp. 4-12. Salt Lake City.

1965 Utah Linguistics and Anasazi Abandonment of the Four Corners Area. In "Contributions of the Wetherill Mesa Archaeological Project," Douglas Osborne, et al. Society for American Archaeology Memoirs, No. 19, pp. 73-81. Washington, D.C.

1968 Culture-Historical Inference from Utaztekan Linguistic Evidence. In "Utaztekan Prehistory," Earl H. Swanson, Jr. (ed.). Idaho State University Museum Occasional Papers, No. 22, pp. 1-42. Pocatello.

GRAHAM, EDWARD EARL

1974 Fremont Dental Pathology and Morphology. Ph.D. dissertation, Department of Anthropology, University of Utah. Salt Lake City.

GRAHAM, EDWARD E., and JOHN BURKART

1976 A Preliminary Analysis of Antemortem Tooth Loss Among the Fremont. American Antiquity, Vol. 41, No. 4, pp. 534-37. Washington, D.C.

GRATER, RUSSEL K.

1955 Appendix I: Grater's Survey. In "Archeology of Zion Park," Albert H. Schroeder. University of Utah Anthropological Papers, No. 22. Salt Lake City.

GREEN, C.H.

1891* Catalogue of a Unique Collection of Cliff Dweller Relics. Privately printed, Chicago.

GREEN, DEE F.

1961 Archaeological Investigations at the G.M. Hinkley Farm Site,

Utah County, Utah, 1956-1960.
Brigham Young University
Press, Provo.

1964 The Hinkley Figurines as Indicators of the Position of Utah Valley in the Sevier Culture. American Antiquity, Vol. 30, No. 1, pp. 74-80. Washington, D.C.

1969 Testing Matheny Alcove, Southeastern Utah. Utah Archeology, Vol. 15, No. 3, pp. 6-9. Salt Lake City.

1970 First Seasons Excavations at Edge of the Cedars Pueblo, Blanding, Utah. Utah Archeology, Vol. 16, No. 2, pp. 1-8. Salt Lake City.

1974 Random Model Testing of Archeological Site Locations in Allen and South Cottonwood Canyons, Southeastern Utah. The Kiva, Vol. 39, Nos. 3-4, pp. 289-99. Tucson.

GREENWOOD, GERALDINE M.

1956 Petroglyphs of the Parowan Valley and Vicinity. In "Archeological Excavations in Iron County, Utah," Clement W. Meighan, et al. University of Utah Anthropological Papers, No. 25, pp. 109-118. Salt Lake City.

GREGORY, HERBERT E.

1916 The Navajo Country, a Geographic and Hydrographic Reconnaissance of Parts of Arizona, New Mexico, and Utah. U.S. Geological Survey Water-supply Paper, No. 380. Washington, D.C.

1938 The San Juan Country: a Geographic and Geologic Reconnaissance of Southeastern Utah. U.S. Geological Survey Professional Papers, No. 188. Washington, D.C.

GREGORY, HERBERT E., and J.C. ANDERSON

1939 Geographic and Geologic Sketch of the Capitol Reef Region, Utah. Geological Society of America Bulletin, No. 50, pp. 1827-50. Chicago.

GROSSCUP, GORDON L.

1962 Excavations in the Hill Creek Area, Grandy County, Utah. Utah Archeology, Vol. 8, No. 3, pp. 3-7. Salt Lake City.

GUNNERSON, D.A.

1956 The Southern Athabascans: Their Arrival in the Southwest. El Palacio, Vol. 63, Nos. 11-12, pp. 346-65. Santa Fe.

GUNNERSON, JAMES H.

1955a University of Utah's Archeological Field Work. Utah Archeology, Vol. 1, No. 3, pp. 3-4. Salt Lake City.

1955b Archeological Evidence of Hunting Magic. Utah Archeology, Vol. 1, No. 3, pp. 5-8. Salt Lake City.

1956a A Fluted Point Site in Utah. American Antiquity, Vol. 21, No. 4, pp. 412-14. Washington, D.C.

1956b Plains-Promontory Relationships. American Antiquity, Vol. 22, No. 1, pp. 69-72. Washington, D.C.

1956c Utah Statewide Survey Activities -- 1955. Utah Archeology, Vol. 2, No. 1, pp. 4-12. Salt Lake City.

1956d Petrographs. Utah Archeology, Vol. 2, No. 2, pp. 11-15. Salt Lake City.

1956e 1956 Archeological Activities of the University of Utah. Utah Archeology, Vol. 2, No. 3, pp. 4-14. Salt Lake City.

1956f   Fremont Ceramics. <u>In</u> "Papers of the Third Great Basin Archeological Conference," Fay Cooper Cole, et al. <u>University of Utah Anthropological Papers</u>, No. 26, pp. 54–62. Salt Lake City.

1957a   An Archeological Survey of the Fremont Area. <u>University of Utah Anthropological Papers</u>, No. 28. Salt Lake City.

1957b   Uinta Basin Archeology. <u>In</u> "Guidebook to the Geology of the Uinta Basin," Otto G. Seal (ed.). <u>Eighth Annual Field Conference, Intermountain Association of Petroleum Geologists</u>, pp. 15–16. Salt Lake City.

1957c   Preliminary Report of 1957 Work at Snake Rock. <u>Utah Archeology</u>, Vol. 3, No. 4, pp. 7–12. Salt Lake City.

1957d   Prehistoric Figurines from Castle Valley. <u>Archaeology</u>, Vol. 10, No. 2, pp. 137–40. Brattleboro.

1958a   <u>Archeological Survey of the Woodruff Narrows Reservoir, Uinta County, Wyoming</u>. MS, Department of Anthropology, University of Utah. Salt Lake City.

1958b   <u>Archeological Survey of the Proposed Dead Horse Point-Junction Butte Utah State Park</u>. MS, Department of Anthropology, University of Utah. Salt Lake City.

1958c   Kaiparowits Plateau Archeological Survey -- a Preliminary Report. <u>Utah Archeology</u>, Vol. 4, No. 3, pp. 9–20. Salt Lake City.

1959a   An Enigmatic Unfired Clay Disk. <u>El Palacio</u>, Vol. 66, No. 3, pp. 107–108. Santa Fe.

1959b   Archaeological Survey in Northeastern New Mexico. <u>El Palacio</u>, Vol. 66, No. 5, pp. 145–54. Santa Fe.

1959c   Archeological Survey in the Dead Horse Point Area. <u>Utah Archeology</u>, Vol. 5, No. 2, pp. 4–9. Salt Lake City.

1959d   Archeological Survey of the Kaiparowits Plateau. <u>In</u> "The Glen Canyon Archeological Survey, Part II," Don D. Fowler, et al. <u>University of Utah Anthropological Papers</u>, No. 39, <u>Glen Canyon Series</u>, No. 6, pp. 319–469. Salt Lake City.

1959e   1957 Excavations, the Glen Canyon Area. <u>University of Utah Anthropological Papers</u>, No. 43. Salt Lake City.

1960a   <u>Archeological Excavations at Snake Rock, Central Utah</u>. MS, Department of Anthropology, University of Utah. Salt Lake City.

1960b   The Fremont Culture: Internal Dimensions and External Relationships. <u>American Antiquity</u>, Vol. 25, No. 3, pp. 373–80. Washington, D.C.

1960c   An Introduction to Plains Apache Archaeology -- the Dismal River Aspect. <u>Bureau of American Ethnology Bulletin</u>, No. 173, <u>Anthropological Paper</u>, No. 58, pp. 131–260. Washington, D.C.

1960d   <u>Fremont Pottery</u>. MS, Department of Anthropology, University of Utah. Salt Lake City.

1962a   Plateau Shoshonean Prehistory: a Suggested Reconstruction. <u>American Antiquity</u>, Vol. 28, No. 1, pp. 41–45. Salt Lake City.

1962b Three Wooden Shovels from Nine Mile Canyon. _University of Utah Anthropological Papers_, No. 60, _Miscellaneous Collected Papers_, pp. 1-8. Salt Lake City.

1962c Archeological Survey in the Hammond Canyon Area, Southeastern Utah. _University of Utah Anthropological Papers_, No. 60, _Miscellaneous Collected Papers_, pp. 9-44. Salt Lake City.

1962d Highway Salvage Archeology: St. George, Utah. _University of Utah Anthropological Papers_, No. 60, _Miscellaneous Collected Papers_, pp. 47-65. Salt Lake City.

1962e Unusual Artifacts from Castle Valley, Central Utah. _University of Utah Anthropological Papers_, No. 60, _Miscellaneous Collected Papers_, pp. 67-91. Salt Lake City.

1969   The Fremont Culture: a Study in Culture Dynamics on the Northern Anasazi Frontier. _Peabody Museum of American Archaeology and Ethnology, Harvard University, Papers_, Vol. 59, No. 2. Cambridge.

n.d.* _Preliminary Report of Archeological Activities During 1955, Department of Anthropology, University of Utah._ Report, Midwest Archeological Center. Lincoln.

GUNNERSON, JAMES H., et al.

1959   Findings. _In_ "The Glen Canyon Archeological Survey, Part I," Don D. Fowler, et al. _University of Utah Anthropological Papers_, No. 39, _Glen Canyon Series_, No. 6, pp. 14-26. Salt Lake City.

"H"

1894* Recent Finds in Utah. _The Archaeologist_, Vol. 2, pp. 154-55. Waterloo.

HAGEMAN, WARREN C.

1961   Artifacts from a Site in Box Elder County, Utah. _Utah Archeology_, Vol. 7, No. 4, pp. 1-5. Salt Lake City.

HALL, HENRY JOHNSON

1969* _Rehydration and Concentration of Parasite Ova in Human Coprolites from the Great Basin._ BA Honors thesis, Department of Anthropology, University of Utah. Salt Lake City.

1970   _An Archeological Survey of the Dixie Reclamation Project._ Report to the National Park Service. MS, Department of Anthropology, University of Utah. Salt Lake City.

1972   _Diet and Disease at Clydes Cavern, Utah: as Revealed Via Paleoscatology._ MA thesis, Department of Anthropology, University of Utah. Salt Lake City.

1973   The Excavation of Zero Plaza. _In_ "Highway U-95 Archeology: Comb Wash to Grand Flat," Gardiner F. Dalley (ed.). _A Special Report_, pp. 63-75. Department of Anthropology, University of Utah. Salt Lake City.

HAMMOND, PHILIP C., and JOHN P. MARWITT

1969   _An Archeometric Survey of Anasazi Indian Village Historical Site, Boulder, Utah._ MS, Department of Anthropology, University of Utah. Salt Lake City.

HANSEN, GEORGE H.

1928   Hairy Mammoth Skeleton in Utah. <u>Science</u>, Vol. 68, p. 621. Washington, D.C.

1934   Utah Lake Skull Cap. <u>American Anthropologist</u>, Vol. 36, No. 3, pp. 431-33. Washington, D.C. Also, <u>Utah Archeology</u>, Vol. 21, No. 1, pp. 21-22. Salt Lake City.

HARDY, DEE

1975   <u>A Description and Analysis of the Architecture and Artifacts of the Picket Fork Sites, Cedar Mesa, San Juan County, Utah</u>. MA thesis, Department of Anthropology, Brigham Young University. Provo.

HARGRAVE, LYNDON L.

1935   <u>Report on Archaeological Reconnaissance in the Rainbow Plateau Area of Northern Arizona and Southern Utah, Bulletin 2</u>. University of California Press, Berkeley.

1936   Notes of a Red Ware from Bluff, Utah. <u>Southwestern Lore</u>, Vol. 2, No. 2, pp. 29-34. Boulder.

1960   Appendix II: Identification of Archeological Feathers from Glen Canyon, Utah. <u>In</u> "1958 Excavations, Glen Canyon Area," William D. Lipe. <u>University of Utah Anthropological Papers</u>, No. 44, <u>Glen Canyon Series</u>, No. 11, pp. 239-41. Salt Lake City.

1961   Appendix I: Bird Bones from the Coombs Site. <u>In</u> "The Coombs Site, Part III: Summary and Conclusions," Robert H. Lister and Florence C. Lister. <u>University of Utah Anthropological Papers</u>, No. 41, <u>Glen Canyon Series</u>, No. 8, pp. 114-16. Salt Lake City.

1970*   Feathers from Sand Dune Cave: a Basketmaker Cave Near Navajo Mountain, Utah. <u>Museum of Northern Arizona Technical Series</u>, No. 9. Flagstaff.

HARLAN, THOMAS P., and JEFFREY S. DEAN

1969*   Appendix II: Tree-Ring Data for Several Navajo Mountain Region Sites. <u>In</u> "Survey and Excavations North and East of Navajo Mountain, 1959-1962," Alexander J. Lindsay, Jr., et al. <u>Museum of Northern Arizona Bulletin</u>, No. 45, pp. 379-82. Flagstaff.

HARPER, KIMBALL T.

1967   The Vegetational Environment of the Bear River No. 2 Archeological Site. <u>In</u> "Excavations at Snake Rock Village and the Bear River No. 2 Site," C. Melvin Aikens. <u>University of Utah Anthropological Papers</u>, No. 87, pp. 63-65. Salt Lake City.

n.d.   <u>Biotic Relations of the Environs of Hogup Cave and Its Deposits</u>. MS, Department of Anthropology, University of Utah. Salt Lake City.

HARPER, KIMBALL T., and G.M. ALDER

1970   Appendix I: The Macroscopic Plant Remains of the Deposits of Hogup Cave, Utah, and Their Paleoclimatic Implications. <u>In</u> "Hogup Cave," C. Melvin Aikens. <u>University of Utah Anthropological Papers</u>, No. 93, pp. 215-40. Salt Lake City.

1972   Paleoclimatic Inferences Concerning the Last 10,000 Years from a Resampling of Danger Cave, Utah. <u>In</u> "Great Basin Cultural Ecology," Don D. Fowler (ed.). <u>Desert Research Institute Publications in the Social Sciences</u>, No. 8. Reno.

HARPER, KIMBALL T., and S.D. DURRANT

1969*   Faunal and Floral Remains as
        Indicators of Neothermal
        Climates at Hogup Cave. Paper
        presented at Society for
        American Archaeology Meeting,
        1969, Milwaukee.

HASSEL, FRANCIS K.

1960   Archeological Notes on the
        Northeastern Margin of Great
        Salt Lake. Utah Archeology,
        Vol. 6, No. 3, pp. 10-15.
        Salt Lake City.

1964   Surface Material from a Site
        in Weber County, Utah. Utah
        Archeology, Vol. 10, No. 3,
        pp. 1-3. Salt Lake City.

1967   A Handled Olla from Injun
        Creek Site (42Wb34). Utah
        Archeology, Vol. 12, No. 2,
        pp. 8-9. Salt Lake City.

HASSEL, FRANCIS K., and CAROL HASSEL

1961   An Open Site near Plain City,
        Utah. Utah Archeology, Vol. 7,
        No. 2, pp. 5-13. Salt Lake
        City.

HAUCK, PAUL A.

1955   Ute Rorschach Performances
        and Some Notes on Field Pro-
        blems and Methods. University
        of Utah Anthropological Papers,
        No. 23. Salt Lake City.

HAUCK, F. RICHARD

1975*   An Archeological Report on
        the Lost Creek Chaining Pro-
        ject. Archeological-Environ-
        mental Research Corporation
        Papers, No. 1. Salt Lake City.

1976a* Archeological Reconnaissance
        in the Dog Valley Locality of
        Emery County, Utah. Archeo-
        gical-Environmental Research
        Corporation Papers, No. 3.
        Salt Lake City.

1976b* An Archeological Survey of the
        Banning Railroad Siding Local-
        ity in Carbon County, Utah.
        Report to the Soldier Creek
        Company. MS, Archeological-
        Environmental Research Corpor-
        ation. Salt Lake City.

1977a* Archeological Reconnaissance in
        Nine Mile Canyon Locality of
        Carbon County, Utah. Archeo-
        logical-Environmental Research
        Corporation Papers, No. 6.
        Salt Lake City.

1977b* Archeological Clearance of an
        Access Route and Two Drill
        Pads in Six Mile Canyon near
        Sterling, Utah. Report to the
        Coastal States Energy Company.
        MS, Archeological-Environmental
        Research Corporation. Salt
        Lake City.

1977c* Archeological Clearance of a
        Pipeline Corridor and Access
        Roads in the Jack Creek Local-
        ity near Nine Mile Canyon in
        Carbon County, Utah. Report to
        Wesco Gas Service. MS,
        Archeological-Environmental
        Research Corporation. Salt
        Lake City.

1977d* Archeological Clearance of
        Support Facilities and Right-
        of-Way at the Wilberg Mine on
        Grimes Creek in Emery County,
        Utah. Report to Utah Power and
        Light Company. MS, Archeologi-
        cal-Environmental Research
        Corporation. Salt Lake City.

HAUCK, F.R., V.G. NORMAN and D.E. WEDER

1977*   An Archeological Survey of 270
        Acres in the Shitamaring/Lost
        Spring Area of the Henry
        Mountains Locality in Garfield
        County, Utah. Report to Pla-
        teau Resources, Ltd. MS,
        Archeological-Environmental
        Research Corporation. Salt
        Lake City.

HAUCK, F.R., and DENNIS E. WEDER

1977*   An Archeological Survey of
        Access Roads and a Mine Ser-
        vice Area in the Ferron Creek
        Locality of Emery County, Utah.
        Report to Canyon Fuel Company
        and Inspiration Consolidated
        Copper Company. MS, Archeolo-
        gical-Environmental Research
        Corporation. Salt Lake City.

HAUCK, F.R., et al.

n.d.*   Archeological Reconnaissance
        in the Paradise Lake Locality
        of Sevier County, Utah.
        Archeological-Environmental
        Research Corporation Papers,
        No. 7, in preparation. Salt
        Lake City.

HAWLEY, FLORENCE M.

1936   Field Manual of Prehistoric
        Southwestern Pottery Types.
        University of New Mexico
        Anthropological Series,
        Bulletin 291, Vol. 1, No. 4.
        Albuquerque.

HAYDEN, IRWIN

1930*   Preliminary Report on Two
        Caves in Southwestern Utah,
        Explored in July and August,
        1930, by the Van Bergen-Los
        Angeles Museum Field Party.
        MS, Los Angeles County Museum.
        Los Angeles. Also, MS, Museum
        of Northern Arizona. Flagstaff.

HEIZER, R.F. (ed.)

1954   Notes on the Utah Utes by
        Edward A. Palmer, 1866-1877.
        University of Utah Anthro-
        pological Papers, No. 17.
        Salt Lake City.

HELM, CLAUDIA F.

1973   Preliminary Report of an
        Archeological Survey in Eastern
        Utah. MS, Department of Anthro-
        pology, University of Utah.
        Salt Lake City.

1974   Preliminary Report of an
        Archeological Survey in Sevier,
        Emery and Garfield Counties,
        Eastern Utah. A Special Report.
        Department of Anthropology,
        University of Utah. Salt Lake
        City.

HENDERSON, RANDALL

1946a   Glyph Hunters in the Indian
        Country. Desert Magazine,
        Vol. 10, No. 1, pp. 11-16.
        Palm Desert.

1946b   We Explored Dark Canyon.
        Desert Magazine, Vol. 10, No.
        2, pp. 5-9. Palm Desert.

1949   Nineteen Days on Utah Trails.
        Desert Magazine, Vol. 12, No.
        13, pp. 5-11; Vol. 13, No. 13,
        pp. 19-25. Palm Desert.

1957   We Camped in the Land of the
        Standing Rocks. Desert Maga-
        zine, Vol. 20, No. 10, pp.
        5-11. Palm Desert.

HEROLD, JOYCE

1961   Prehistoric Settlement and
        Physical Environment in the
        Mesa Verde Area. University
        of Utah Anthropological Papers,
        No. 53. Salt Lake City.

HESSION, EDWIN A., and FREDERICK P.
FRAMPTON

1974*   Phase I Archaeological and
        Environmental Research:
        Kaiparowits Power Project,
        Arizona Public Service, Kai-
        parowits to Westwing Power
        Line. MS, Museum of Northern
        Arizona. Flagstaff.

HESTER, THOMAS R.

1970   Chronological Ordering of
        Great Basin Prehistory. Con-
        tributions of the University
        of California Archaeological
        Research Facility, No. 27.
        Berkeley.

HESTER, THOMAS R., and ROBERT F. HEIZER

1973   Review and Discussion of Great
        Basin Projectile Points: Form
        and Chronology. University of
        California Archaeological Re-
        search Facility, Berkeley.

HEWETT, E.L.

n.d.*   Field Notes, 1906-1909. MS,
        Midwest Archeological Center.
        Lincoln.

HILL, W.W.

1938   The Agricultural and Hunting
        Methods of the Navaho Indians.
        Yale University Publications
        in Anthropology, Vol. 18,
        pp. 1-194. New Haven.

HOBLER, PHILIP M.

1962   An Archeological Survey in the
        Upper White River Basin, South-
        eastern Utah. MS, Department
        of Anthropology, University of
        Utah. Salt Lake City.

1974   The Late Survival of Pithouse
        Architecture in the Kayenta
        Anasazi Area. Southwestern
        Lore, Vol. 40, No. 2, pp. 1-
        44. Boulder.

n.d.   Archeological Survey of Pro-
        posed Access Road, Natural
        Bridges National Monument.
        Report, Midwest Archeological
        Center. Lincoln.

HOGAN, PATRICK F., and RICHARD N.
HOLMER

1975a   Survey of Archeological and
        Historical Resources within
        the Jensen Unit of the Central
        Utah Project. Report to the
        National Park Service. MS,
        Department of Anthropology,
        University of Utah. Salt Lake
        City.

1976b   Survey of Archeological and
        Historical Resources within
        the Uintah Unit of the Central
        Utah Project. Report to the
        National Park Service. MS, De-
        partment of Anthropology, Uni-
        versity of Utah. Salt Lake City.

HOGAN, PATRICK F., LEONARD LOSEE and
JAMES DODGE

1975   Archeological Investigations in
        the Maze District, Canyonlands
        National Park, Utah. MS, Depart-
        ment of Anthropology, Univer-
        sity of Utah. Salt Lake City.

HOLLIMAN, R.B.

1969   Further Studies on Incised
        Stones from the Great Salt Lake
        Desert, Utah. Southwestern Lore,
        Vol. 35, No. 2, pp. 23-25.
        Boulder.

HOLMER, RICHARD N.

1975a   Report of the Archeological Ex-
        cavation on the Brigham Young
        Forest Farm Site. Report to the
        Utah State Division of Parks
        and Recreation. MS, Department
        of Anthropology, University of
        Utah. Salt Lake City.

1975b   Survey of Archeological and
        Historical Resources within
        the Bonneville Unit of the
        Central Utah Project. Report
        to the National Park Service.
        MS, Department of Anthropology,
        University of Utah. Salt Lake
        City.

1976a   Survey of Archeological and
        Historical Resources within
        the Alpine Aquaduct Area of the
        Central Utah Project. Report to
        the National Park Service. MS,

Department of Anthropology, University of Utah. Salt Lake City.

1976b Survey of Archeological and Historical Resources within the Provo Reservoir Canal Area of the Central Utah Project. Report to the National Park Service. MS, Department of Anthropology, University of Utah. Salt Lake City.

1976c Test Excavation within the Uintah Unit of the Central Utah Project: Site 42Un435. Report to the National Park Service. MS, Department of Anthropology, University of Utah. Salt Lake City.

1976d Survey of Archeological and Historical Resources within the Strawberry Reservoir Area of the Central Utah Project. Report to the National Park Service. MS, Department of Anthropology, University of Utah. Salt Lake City.

1976e Projectile Points. In "Sudden Shelter," Jesse D. Jennings, Alan R. Schroedl and Richard N. Holmer. University of Utah Anthropological Papers, in press. Salt Lake City.

1977   Archeological Survey of Exxon Mineral Leases, Lake Mead National Recreation Area. Report to the National Park Service. MS, Department of Anthropology, University of Utah. Salt Lake City.

1978   A Mathematical Typology for Archaic Projectile Points of the Eastern Great Basin. Ph.D. dissertation, Department of Anthropology, University of Utah. Salt Lake City.

n.d.   Projectile Points. In "Cowboy Cave," Jesse D. Jennings. University of Utah Anthropological Papers, in preparation. Salt Lake City.

HOLMES, W.H.

1878   Report on the Ancient Ruins of Southwestern Colorado, Examined During the Summers of 1875 and 1876. U.S. Geological and Geographical Survey of the Territories for 1876, 10th Annual Report, pp. 383-408. Washington, D.C.

1886   Pottery of the Ancient Pueblos. Bureau of American Ethnology Annual Reports, No. 4, pp. 257-360. Washington, D.C.

HOPKINS, N.A.

1965   Great Basin Prehistory and Uto-Aztecan. American Antiquity, Vol. 31, No. 1, pp. 48-60. Washington, D.C.

HRDLICKA, ALES

1908   Physiological and Medical Observations Among the Indians of Southwestern United States and Northern Mexico. Bureau of American Ethnology Bulletin, No. 34. Washington, D.C.

1931   Catalogue of Human Crania in the United States National Museum Collections: Pueblos, Southern Utah Basket-makers, Navaho. United States National Museum Proceedings, No. 78, pp. 1-95.

HULL, DEBBIE

1977* Bibliography of References in Southwestern Colorado. MS, Midwest Archeological Center. Lincoln.

HULL, FRANK W.

1976a   A Survey of Archeological and
         Historical Resources within
         the Bonneville Unit of the
         Central Utah Project: Lower
         Stillwater Recreation Areas.
         Report to the National Park
         Service. MS, Department of
         Anthropology, University of
         Utah. Salt Lake City.

1976b   Survey of Archeological and
         Historical Resources within
         the Upalco Unit of the Central
         Utah Project: Moon Lake En-
         largement. Report to the
         National Park Service. MS,
         Department of Anthropology,
         University of Utah. Salt Lake
         City.

1976c   Survey of Archeological and
         Historical Resources within
         the Bonneville Unit of the
         Central Utah Project: Mona
         Complex. Report to the National
         Park Service. MS, Department of
         Anthropology, University of
         Utah. Salt Lake City.

1976d   Survey of Archeological and
         Historical Resources within
         the Upalco Unit of the Central
         Utah Project: Taskeech Reser-
         voir Recreation Sites. Report
         to the National Park Service.
         MS, Department of Anthropology,
         University of Utah. Salt Lake
         City.

1976e   Appendix III: Comparative Pol-
         len Sampling Techniques at
         Remnant Cave. In "Swallow
         Shelter and Associated Sites,"
         Gardiner F. Dalley. University
         of Utah Anthropological Papers,
         No. 96, pp. 175-79. Salt Lake
         City.

HULL, FRANK W., and CRAIG W. FULLER

1976   Survey of Archeological and
         Historical Resources within
         the Bonneville Unit of the Cen-
         tral Utah Project: Deer Creek
         Dam Enlargement. Report to the
         National Park Service. MS,
         Department of Anthropology,
         University of Utah. Salt Lake
         City.

HUNT, ALICE P.

1952   Recommendations for Additional
         Work in the Indian Creek Area,
         San Juan County, Utah. MS,
         Department of Anthropology,
         University of Utah. Salt Lake
         City.

1953   Archeological Survey of the La
         Sal Mountain Area, Utah. Uni-
         versity of Utah Anthropological
         Papers, No. 14. Salt Lake City.

1960   A Sketch of Utah Prehistory.
         Utah Archeology, Vol. 6, No. 1,
         pp. 4-14. Salt Lake City.

HUNT, ALICE P., and DALLAS TANNER

1960   Early Man Sites near Moab, Utah.
         American Antiquity, Vol. 26,
         No. 1, pp. 110-17. Washington,
         D.C.

HUNT, ALICE P., and BATES WILSON

1952   Archeological Sites in the
         Horse Canyon Area, San Juan
         County, Utah. MS, Department of
         Anthropology, University of
         Utah. Salt Lake City.

HUNT, CHARLES B.

1967   Henry Mountains. MS, Department
         of Anthropology, University of
         Utah. Salt Lake City.

HUSTED, W.M., and O.L. MALLORY

1967   The Fremont Culture: Its Deri-
         vation and Ultimate Fate.
         Plains Anthropologist, Vol. 12,
         pp. 222-32. Lincoln.

JACKSON, WILLIAM H.

1876a Ancient Ruins in Southwestern Colorado. U.S. Geological and Geographical Survey of the Territories for 1874, 8th Annual Report, pp. 367-81. Washington, D.C.

1876b* Notice of Ancient Ruins in Arizona and Utah Lying About the Rio San Juan. U.S. Geological and Geographical Survey of the Territories for 1874, 8th Annual Report, Bulletin II, No. 2. Washington, D.C.

1878 Report on Ancient Ruins Examined in 1875 and 1877. U.S. Geological and Geographical Survey of the Territories for 1876, 10th Annual Report, pp. 411-50. Washington, D.C.

JAMESON, SYDNEY

1948 Archeological Notes on Stansbury Island, Utah. MS thesis, University of Utah Library. Also, University of Utah Anthropological Papers, No. 34 (1958). Salt Lake City.

JARVIS, L., R. LISENBY, and C. SIVERO

1964* 1964 Excavations at Summit, Utah: a Progress Report. MS, Department of Anthropology, University of California at Los Angeles. Los Angeles.

JENNINGS, CALVIN H.

1967* Archaeological Reconnaissance in the Paria Canyon, Arizona-Utah, 1967. MS, Museum of Northern Arizona. Flagstaff.

JENNINGS, JESSE D.

1951 Report of the Preliminary Archeological Reconnaissance of the Kaiparowits Plateau, Kane County, Utah. MS, Department of Anthropology, University of Utah. Salt Lake City.

1953 Danger Cave: a Progress Summary. El Palacio, Vol. 60, No. 5, pp. 179-213. Santa Fe.

1956a Radiocarbon Dates from Danger Cave. Utah Archeology, Vol. 2, No. 2, pp. 3-6. Salt Lake City.

1956b Early Man in the West. Utah Archeology, Vol. 2, No. 3, pp. 2-5. Salt Lake City.

1956c The American Southwest: a Problem in Cultural Isolation. Society for American Archaeology Memoirs, No. 11, pp. 59-128. Washington, D.C.

1957a Upper Colorado River Basin Archeological Salvage Project: Summer 1957. Utah Archeology, Vol. 3, No. 3, pp. 7-9. Salt Lake City.

1957b Danger Cave. University of Utah Anthropological Papers, No. 27. Salt Lake City. Also, Society for American Archaeology Memoirs, No. 14. Washington, D.C.

1959 Introductory History. In "The Glen Canyon Archeological Survey, Part I," Don D. Fowler, et al. University of Utah Anthropological Papers, No. 39, Glen Canyon Series, No. 6, pp. 1-13. Salt Lake City.

1960 Early Man in Utah. Utah Historical Quarterly, Vol. 28, No. 1, pp. 3-27. Salt Lake City.

1963 Computers and Culture History: a Glen Canyon Study. Paper presented at American Anthropological Association Meeting, San Francisco. MS, Department of Anthropology, University of Utah. Salt Lake City.

1964a The Glen Canyon: a Multi-Discipline Project, or, Something for Everybody. Paper presented at University of Utah Faculty Seminar, 1964. MS, Department of Anthropology, University of Utah. Salt Lake City.

1964b The Desert West. In *Prehistoric Man in the New World*, Jesse D. Jennings and Edward Norbeck (eds.), pp. 149–74. University of Chicago Press, Chicago.

1966a Early Man in the Desert West. *Quaternaria*, Vol. 8, pp. 81–89. Rome.

1966b Glen Canyon: a Summary. *University of Utah Anthropological Papers*, No. 81, *Glen Canyon Series*, No. 31. Salt Lake City.

1968 The Prehistory of North America. *McGraw-Hill, New York.*

1970 Canyonlands – aborigines. *Natural History Society of Minnesota Special Issues, Naturalist*, Vol. 21, No. 2, pp. 12–15. Minneapolis.

1974 The Prehistory of North America. 2d edition. McGraw-Hill, New York.

1975a *Preliminary Report: Excavation of Cowboy Caves, June 3 – July 26, 1975*. MS, Department of Anthropology, University of Utah. Salt Lake City.

1975b *Desert Dwellers with Few Resources: 10,000 Years of Utah Prehistory*. Leigh Lecture, 1975. MS, Department of Anthropology, University of Utah. Salt Lake City.

1975c *A Brief Summary of Utah Prehistory*. MS, Department of Anthropology, University of Utah. Salt Lake City.

1976 *Preliminary Report: 1976 Archeological Excavation, Bull Creek Area*. MS, Department of Anthropology, University of Utah. Salt Lake City.

1977 *Preliminary Report: 1977 Archeological Excavation, Bull Creek Area*. MS, Department of Anthropology, University of Utah. Salt Lake City.

1978 Prehistory of Utah and the Eastern Great Basin. *University of Utah Anthropological Papers*, No. 98. Salt Lake City.

n.d.a *Index of Petroglyphs and Pictographs in Utah*. MS, Department of Anthropology, University of Utah. Salt Lake City.

n.d.b Cowboy Cave. *University of Utah Anthropological Papers*, in preparation. Salt Lake City.

(ED.)

1950 Proceedings of the Sixth Plains Archeological Conference, 1948. *University of Utah Anthropological Papers*, No. 11. Salt Lake City.

JENNINGS, JESSE D., and GARDINER F. DALLEY

1972 *Report of Preliminary Archeological Survey of the Kaiparowits Plateau Region, Southeastern Utah*. Report to Bechtel Corporation, Los Angeles. MS, Department of Anthropology, University of Utah. Salt Lake City.

JENNINGS, JESSE D., and EDWARD NORBECK

1955 Great Basin Prehistory: a Review. *American Antiquity*, Vol. 21, No. 1, pp. 1–11. Washington, D.C.

JENNINGS, JESSE D., ALAN R. SCHROEDL and RICHARD N. HOLMER

1976 Sudden Shelter. *University of Utah Anthropological Papers*, in press. Salt Lake City.

JENNINGS, JESSE D., and FLOYD W. SHARROCK

1965 The Glen Canyon: a Multi-Discipline Project. *Utah Historical Quarterly*, Vol. 33, No. 1, pp. 35–50. Salt Lake City.

JOHNSON, ROBERT L.

1976   A Comprehensive Survey and
        Analysis of the San Rafael
        Fremont Ceramic Industry: the
        Emery County (Utah) Area. MA
        thesis, Department of Anthro-
        pology, University of Nebras-
        ka. Lincoln.

JONES, CARL H.

1958   A Puebloid Site in Utah Valley.
        Utah Archeology, Vol. 4, No.
        2, pp. 7-13. Salt Lake City.

1961*   An Archaeological Survey of
        Utah County, Utah. MA thesis,
        Department of Anthropology,
        Brigham Young University.
        Provo.

JONES, VOLNEY H.

n.d.*   Plant Materials from Fremont
        Sites, Sevier County, Utah.
        Ethnobotanical Laboratory
        Report, No. 376. University of
        Michigan, Ann Arbor.

JUDD, NEIL M.

1916   Archaeological Reconnaissance
        in Western Utah. Smithsonian
        Miscellaneous Collections,
        Vol. 66, No. 3, pp. 64-71.
        Washington, D.C.

1917a   Archaeological Reconnaissance
        in Western Utah. Smithsonian
        Miscellaneous Collections,
        Vol. 66, No. 17, pp. 103-108.
        Washington, D.C.

1917b   Notes on Certain Prehistoric
        Habitations in Western Utah.
        19th International Congress
        of Americanists, Proceedings,
        pp. 119-24. Washington, D.C.

1917c   Evidence of Circular Kivas in
        Western Utah Ruins. American
        Anthropologist, Vol. 19, pp.
        34-40. Washington, D.C.

1918   Archaeological Work in Arizona
        and Utah. Smithsonian Miscel-
        laneous Collections, Vol. 68,
        No. 12, pp. 74-83. Washing-
        ton, D.C.

1919   Archaeological Investigations
        of Paragonah, Utah. Smithson-
        ian Miscellaneous Collections,
        Vol. 70, No. 3, pp. 1-22.
        Washington, D.C.

1920   Archaeological Investigations
        in Utah and Arizona. Smithson-
        ian Miscellaneous Collections,
        Vol. 72, No. 1, pp. 66-69.
        Washington, D.C.

1921*   Archaeological Investigations
        in Utah, Arizona and New Mexi-
        co. Smithsonian Miscellaneous
        Collections, Vol. 72, No. 6,
        pp. 96-102. Washington, D.C.

1924a* Explorations in San Juan
        County, Utah. Smithsonian
        Miscellaneous Collections,
        Vol. 76, No. 10, pp. 77-81.
        Washington, D.C.

1924b   Beyond the Clay Hills. Nation-
        al Geographic, Vol. 45, No. 3,
        pp. 276-302. Washington, D.C.

1926   Archaeological Observations
        North of the Rio Colorado.
        Bureau of American Ethnology
        Bulletin, No. 82. Washington,
        D.C.

1927*   The Discovery of Rainbow
        Bridge. National Parks
        Bulletin, Vol. 9, No. 54,
        pp. 7-16. Washington, D.C.

KAY, MARVIN

1973*   Archeological Road Surveys in
        Canyonlands and Capitol Reef
        National Parks and Adjacent
        Bureau of Land Management
        Areas, Wayne and Garfield
        Counties, Utah. Report, Mid-
        west Archeological Center.
        Lincoln.

1974* Archeological Reconnaissance within Glen Canyon National Recreation Area, Arizona and Utah. Report, Midwest Archeological Center. Lincoln.

KAYSER, JOYCE

1965 Phantoms in the Pinyons: an Investigation of Ute-Pueblo Contacts. Society for American Archaeology Memoirs, No. 19. Washington, D.C.

KELLER, GORDON N., and JOHN D. HUNT

1967 Lithic Materials from Escalante Valley, Utah. University of Utah Anthropological Papers, No. 89, Miscellaneous Papers, No. 17, pp. 53-59. Salt Lake City.

KELLEY, CHARLES

1943 We Found a Gallery of Indian Etchings. Desert Magazine, Vol. 6, No. 11, pp. 18-19. Palm Desert.

1945a* Archeological Research in Capitol Reef National Monument. In Charles Kelley's Writings on Capitol Reef National Monument. MS, Capitol Reef National Park.

1945b* Petroglyphs of Capitol Reef National Monument. In Charles Kelley's Writings on Capitol Reef National Monument. MS, Capitol Reef National Park.

1950 Murals Painted by Ancient Tribesmen. Desert Magazine, Vol. 13, No. 8, pp. 11-12. Palm Desert.

KELLY, ISABEL T.

1934 Southern Paiute Bands. American Anthropologist, Vol. 36, pp. 548-60. Washington, D.C.

1939 Southern Paiute Shamanism. University of California

Anthropological Records, Vol. 2, No. 4, pp. 151-57. Berkeley.

1964 Southern Paiute Ethnography. University of Utah Anthropological Papers, No. 69, Glen Canyon Series, No. 21. Salt Lake City.

KELSO, GERALD

1970 Appendix IV: Hogup Cave, Utah: Comparative Pollen Analysis of Human Coprolites and Cave Fill. In "Hogup Cave," C. Melvin Aikens. University of Utah Anthropological Papers, No. 93. Salt Lake City.

KIDDER, ALFRED V.

1910 Explorations in Southwestern Utah in 1908. American Journal of Archaeology, 2d Series, Vol. 14, No. 3, pp. 337-60. Norwood.

1917 Prehistoric Cultures of the San Juan Drainage. 19th International Congress of Americanists, Proceedings. Washington, D.C.

1924 An Introduction to the Study of Southwestern Archaeology, with a Preliminary Account of the Excavations at Pecos. Phillips Academy Southwestern Expedition Papers, No. 1. Yale University Press, New Haven.

1936 The Archaeology of Peripheral Regions. Southwestern Lore, Vol. 2, No. 3, pp. 46-48. Boulder.

KIDDER, ALFRED V., and SAMUEL J. GUERNSEY

1919 Archaeological Explorations in Northeastern Arizona. Bureau of American Ethnology Bulletin, No. 65. Washington, D. C.

KING, T.G.

1893* An Exploration of the Region Occupied by the Cliff-Dwellers. The Archaeologist, Vol. 1, No. 6, pp. 100-105.

KOWTA, MARY M.

1963 An Archeological Survey of Capitol Reef National Monument. MS, Department of Anthropology, University of Utah. Salt Lake City.

KRIEGER, ALEX D.

1950 A Suggested General Sequence in North American Projectile Points. In "Proceedings of the Sixth Plains Archeological Conference, 1948," Jesse D. Jennings (ed.). University of Utah Anthropological Papers, No. 11, pp. 117-24. Salt Lake City.

1962 The Earliest Cultures in the Western United States. American Antiquity, Vol. 28, No. 2, pp. 138-43. Washington, D.C.

1964 Early Man in the New World. In Prehistoric Man in the New World, Jesse D. Jennings and Edward Norbeck (eds.), pp. 23-81. University of Chicago Press, Chicago.

LAMB, SIDNEY M.

1958 Linguistic Prehistory in the Great Basin. International Journal of American Linguistics, Vol. 24, No. 2, pp. 95-100. Baltimore.

LANCE, J.F.
1963 Alluvial Stratigraphy in Lake and Moqui Canyons. In "1961 Excavations, Glen Canyon Area," Floyd W. Sharrock, et al. University of Utah Anthropological Papers, No. 63, Glen Canyon Series, No. 18. Salt Lake City.

LANG, GOTTFRIED O.

1953 A Study in Culture Contact and Culture Change: the Whiterock Utes in Transition. University of Utah Anthropological Papers, No. 15. Salt Lake City.

LEACH, LARRY L.

1966a* Excavation of Swelter Shelter, Site 42Un40, Dinosaur National Monument. MS, Anthropology Laboratory, University of Colorado. Boulder.

1966b The Archeology of Boundary Village. University of Utah Anthropological Papers, No. 83, Miscellaneous Papers, No. 13. Salt Lake City.

1967 Archaeological Investigations at Deluge Shelter (42Un1). Report to the National Park Service. MS, University of Colorado. Boulder. MS, Dinosaur National Monument.

1970 Archaeological Investigations at Deluge Shelter (42Un1). Ph.D. dissertation, University of Colorado. Boulder.

LEH, LEONARD L.

1936 Prehistoric Pueblo Ruins in Range Creek Canyon, Utah. University of Colorado Studies, Vol. 23, No. 2, pp. 159-68. Boulder.

1938 Some Surprises at the Wilson Ruins in San Juan County, Utah. Southwestern Lore, Vol. 3, No. 4, pp. 66-69, 72-73. Boulder.

1939 Further Studies at the Wilson Ruins. Southwestern Lore, Vol. 4, No. 4, pp. 68-72. Boulder.

1940 A Prehistoric Population Center in the Southwest. Southwestern Lore, Vol. 6, No. 2, pp. 21-25. Boulder.

1942   A Preliminary Report on the
       Monument Ruins in San Juan
       County, Utah. *University of
       Colorado Studies*, Vol. 1, No.
       3, pp. 261-95. Boulder.

LINDSAY, ALEXANDER J., JR.

1961   The Beaver Creek Agricultural
       Community on the San Juan River,
       Utah. *American Antiquity*, Vol.
       27, No. 2, pp. 174-87. Washing-
       ton, D.C.

1968   *Pottery Pueblo - NA7713, a
       Tsegi Phase Settlement on
       Paiute Mesa, Utah.* MS, Museum
       of Northern Arizona. Flagstaff.

1969   *Burials from Upper Glen Can-
       yon.* MS, Department of Anthro-
       pology, University of Utah.
       Salt Lake City.

LINDSAY, ALEXANDER J., JR., and
J. RICHARD AMBLER

1963   Recent Contributions and Re-
       search Problems in Kayenta
       Anasazi Prehistory. *Plateau*,
       Vol. 35, No. 3, pp. 86-92.
       Flagstaff.

LINDSAY, ALEXANDER J., JR., CHRISTY G.
TURNER II and PAUL V. LONG, JR.

1962   *Archaeological Excavations
       Along Lower San Juan River,
       Utah, 1958-1960.* MS, Museum
       of Northern Arizona. Flagstaff.

LINDSAY, ALEXANDER J., JR., et al.

1968a* Survey and Excavation North and
       East of Navajo Mountain, Utah,
       1959-1962. *Museum of Northern
       Arizona Bulletin*, No. 45.
       Flagstaff.

1968b* *Survey and Excavations on
       Paiute Mesa, 1960-1962.* Report,
       Midwest Archeological Center.
       Lincoln.

LINDSAY, LAMAR W.

1974a *Archeological Survey, Site
       42Gr512, Line Canyon, Dolores
       River Drainage, Grand County,
       Utah.* MS, Department of Anthro-
       pology, University of Utah.
       Salt Lake City.

1974b Report of a Preliminary Archeo-
       logical Survey of Coal Lease
       Lands (U-073039, U-073040, and
       U-073041), Sevier and Emery
       Counties, Utah. *A Special Re-
       port.* Bureau of Land Manage-
       ment, Salt Lake City.

1974c Preliminary Palynological
       Studies on Cedar Mesa. *In*
       "Highway U-95 Archeology: Comb
       Wash to Grand Flat, Vol. II,"
       Curtis J. Wilson (ed.). *A
       Special Report*, pp. 155-176.
       Department of Anthropology,
       University of Utah. Salt Lake
       City.

1975   Appendix V: Palynological Ana-
       lysis and Paleoecology of Inno-
       cents Ridge. *In* "Innocents
       Ridge and the San Rafael Fre-
       mont," Alan R. Schroedl, and
       Patrick F. Hogan. *Antiquities
       Section Selected Papers*, Vol.
       1, No. 2, pp. 61-64. Utah State
       Historical Society, Salt Lake
       City.

1976a *Grand County: an Archeological
       Summary.* MS, Antiquities Sec-
       tion, Utah State Historical
       Society. Salt Lake City.

1976b Unusual or Enigmatic Stone
       Artifacts: Pots, Pipes, Points,
       and Pendants from Utah. *Anti-
       quities Section Selected
       Papers*, Vol. 2, No. 8. Utah
       State Historical Society, Salt
       Lake City.

1976c   Pollen Analysis of Sudden
         Shelter Site Deposits. In
         "Sudden Shelter," Jesse D.
         Jennings, Alan R. Schroedl and
         Richard N. Holmer. University
         of Utah Anthropological Papers,
         in press. Salt Lake City.

LINDSAY, LAMAR W., and RICHARD E. FIKE

1974*   Archeological Survey of Bu-
         reau of Land Management Utah
         State Exchange Lands (U-18819,
         U-18820) on the Bluff Bench
         and (U-18821) on White Mesa,
         San Juan County, Utah. A Spe-
         cial Report. Bureau of Land
         Management, Salt Lake City.

LINDSAY, LAMAR W., and CHRISTIAN K.
LUND

1976   Pint-Size Shelter. Antiquities
         Section Selected Papers, Vol.
         3, No. 10. Utah State Histor-
         ical Society, Salt Lake City.

LINDSAY, LAMAR W., and REX E. MADSEN

1973a   Report of Archeological Survey
         of the LaVerkin Springs Dis-
         posal Facilities (Colorado
         River Water Quality Improve-
         ment Program), Washington
         County, Utah. MS, Department
         of Anthropology, University of
         Utah. Salt Lake City.

1973b   Report of Archeological Sur-
         veys of the Pipe Springs Na-
         tional Monument Water Supply
         System Project: Kaibab Indian
         Reservation, Mohave County,
         Arizona; Zion National Park
         Sewer Extension Project,
         Washington County, Utah;
         Arches National Park Road and
         Sewage Disposal Area Projects,
         Grand County, Utah; and Can-
         yonlands National Park Road
         Projects, Needles and Grand-
         view Point Areas, San Juan
         County, Utah. MS, Department
         of Anthropology, University of
         Utah. Salt Lake City.

1973c   Report of Archeological Survey
         of the Tyzack Dam and Reservoir
         (Jensen Unit) and the Taskeech
         Dam and Reservoir (Upalco Unit)
         Project Areas of the Central
         Utah Project. MS, Department of
         Anthropology, University of
         Utah. Salt Lake City.

1973d   Report of Archeological Survey
         of the Upper Stillwater Dam
         and Reservoir, the Currant
         Creek Dam and Reservoir, and
         the Strawberry Reservoir Pro-
         ject Areas (Bonneville Unit)
         of the Central Utah Project.
         MS, Department of Anthropology,
         University of Utah. Salt Lake
         City.

LIPE, WILLIAM D.

1958   Archeological Excavations in
         Glen Canyon: a Preliminary
         Report of 1958 Work. Utah
         Archeology, Vol. 4, No. 4,
         pp. 4-13. Salt Lake City.

1960a   Archeological Survey of the
         Steinaker Reservoir Area,
         Uintah County, Utah. MS,
         Department of Anthropology,
         University of Utah. Salt Lake
         City.

1960b   1958 Excavations, Glen Canyon
         Area. University of Utah
         Anthropological Papers, No. 44,
         Glen Canyon Series, No. 11.
         Salt Lake City.

1967   Anasazi Culture and its Rela-
         tionship to the Environment in
         the Red Rock Plateau Region,
         Southeastern Utah. Ph.D. dis-
         sertation, Department of
         Anthropology, Yale University.
         New Haven.

1968a   Anasazi Communities of the Red
         Rock Plateau, S.E. Utah.
         Paper presented at the School
         of American Research Advanced
         Seminar, April 1968, Santa Fe.

1968b   Anasazi Settlement Patterns in S.E. Utah. Paper presented at Columbia University Seminar on Ecological Systems and Cultural Evolution.

1968c   Review of Paul V. Long, "Archeological Excavations in Lower Glen Canyon, Utah, 1959-60." American Antiquity, Vol. 33, No. 3, pp. 401-402. Washington, D.C.

1970   Anasazi Communities in the Red Rock Plateau, Southeastern Utah. In Reconstructing Prehistoric Societies, William A. Longacre (ed.), pp. 84-139. University of New Mexico Press, Albuquerque.

1971   Review of John P. Marwitt, "Pharo Village." American Antiquity, Vol. 36, No. 2, pp. 224-25. Washington, D.C.

1973   Review of Lindsay, et al., "Survey and Excavations North and East of Navajo Mountain, Utah." American Antiquity, Vol. 38, No. 2, pp. 243-44. Washington, D.C.

1975a   Archaeology of the Canyonlands Region. Paper presented at Four Corners Geological Society, Eighth Field Conference, Indian Creek State Park, Utah.

1975b   Archaeological Research in the Cedar Mesa Region, S.E. Utah. Public lecture at Fort Lewis College, Durango.

n.d.a   Basketmaker II Sites of the Grand Gulch Region. National Geographic Society Research in 1969, in press.

n.d.b   Grand Gulch: Three Days on the Road from Bluff. Section of a photo-oriented book on Southwestern archaeological sites by Marc and Marnie Gaede.

n.d.c   The Southwest. In Ancient Native Americans, Jesse D. Jennings (ed.), in press. W.H. Freeman, San Francisco.

LIPE, WILLIAM D., and R.G. MATSON

1971   Human Settlement and Resources in the Cedar Mesa Area, S.E. Utah. In "The Distribution of Prehistoric Population Aggregates," George J. Gumerman (ed.). Prescott College Anthropological Reports, No. 1, pp. 126-51. Prescott.

1973a   Regional Sampling: a Case Study from Cedar Mesa, Southeastern Utah. Papers presented at the Symposium on Archaeological Sampling, Society for American Archaeology Meeting, 1973, San Francisco.

1973b* Progress Report on Year I of the Cedar Mesa Project. Progress report to the National Science Foundation. Flagstaff.

1975a   Archeology and Alluvium in the Grand Gulch-Cedar Mesa Area, Southern Utah. In "Four Corners Geological Society Guidebook," pp. 67-71. Eighth Field Conference, Farmington. Also, Utah Archeology, Vol. 21, No. 2, pp. 1-9. Salt Lake City.

1975b   The Cedar Mesa Project. Paper presented at the Symposium on the Wilderness and Cultural Values, Society for American Archaeology Meeting, 1975, Dallas.

1975c   Regional Sampling: a Case Study from Cedar Mesa, Southeastern Utah. In Sampling in Archaeology, James Mueller (ed.), pp. 124-43. University of Arizona Press, Tucon.

1977   Seriation of Cedar Mesa Cera-
        mics. MS, Department of Anthro-
        pology, Washington State Uni-
        versity. Pullman.

n.d.   Settlement Patterns on Cedar
        Mesa: Boom and Bust on the
        Northern Periphery. In "Pro-
        ceedings of the 1976 SARG
        Conference," Robert Euler and
        George Gumerman (eds.).
        Museum of Northern Arizona
        Bulletin, in press. Flagstaff.

LIPE, WILLIAM D., R.G. MATSON and
MARGARET POWERS

1977   Archaeological Sampling Survey
        of Proposed Additions to the
        Existing Grand Gulch Primitive
        Area. MS, Museum of Northern
        Arizona. Flagstaff.

LIPE, WILLIAM D., et al.

1960   1959 Excavations, Glen Canyon
        Area. University of Utah
        Anthropological Papers, No. 49,
        Glen Canyon Series, No. 13.
        Salt Lake City.

LISTER, FLORENCE C.

1959   Pottery. In "The Coombs Site,
        Part I," Robert H. Lister.
        University of Utah Anthropo-
        logical Papers, No. 41, Glen
        Canyon Series, No. 8, pp. 68-
        89. Salt Lake City.

1960   Pottery. In "The Coombs Site,
        Part II," Robert H. Lister,
        J. Richard Ambler and Florence
        C. Lister. University of Utah
        Anthropological Papers, No. 41,
        Glen Canyon Series, No. 8,
        pp. 182-238. Salt Lake City.

1964   Kaiparowits Plateau and Glen
        Canyon Prehistory: an Interpre-
        tation Based on Ceramics.
        University of Utah Anthropolo-
        gical Papers, No. 71, Glen
        Canyon Series, No. 23. Salt
        Lake City.

LISTER, FLORENCE, and ROBERT H. LISTER

1968   Earl Morris and Southwestern
        Archeology. University of New
        Mexico Press, Albuquerque.

LISTER, ROBERT H.

1951   Excavations at Hells Midden,
        Dinosaur National Monument.
        University of Colorado Studies,
        Series in Anthropology, No. 3.
        Boulder.

1958a   The Glen Canyon Survey in 1957.
        University of Utah Anthropo-
        logical Papers, No. 30, Glen
        Canyon Series, No. 1. Salt
        Lake City.

1958b   A Preliminary Note on Excava-
        tions at the Coombs Site,
        Boulder, Utah. Utah Archeology,
        Vol. 4, No. 3, pp. 4-8. Salt
        Lake City.

1959a   The Glen Canyon Right Bank Sur-
        vey. In "The Glen Canyon Arche-
        ological Survey, Part I," Don
        D. Fowler, et al. University
        of Utah Anthropological Papers,
        No. 39, Glen Canyon Series,
        No. 6, pp. 27-162. Salt Lake
        City.

1959b   The Waterpocket Fold: a Distri-
        butional Problem. In "The Glen
        Canyon Archeological Survey,
        Part I," Don D. Fowler, et al.
        University of Utah Anthropolo-
        gical Papers, No. 39, Glen
        Canyon Series, No. 6, pp.
        285-317. Salt Lake City.

1959c   The Coombs Site (Part I).
        University of Utah Anthropolo-
        gical Papers, No. 41, Glen
        Canyon Series, No. 8. Salt
        Lake City.

1960a   Site Testing Program, 1960,
        San Juan Triangle Area and
        Escalante. MS, Department of
        Anthropology, University of
        Utah. Salt Lake City.

1960b   San Juan Triangle Area and
        Escalante, Summary Report. MS,
        Department of Anthropology,
        University of Utah. Salt Lake
        City.

1962   Salvage Archeology in the
        Colorado Region of Northern
        Arizona and Southern Utah.
        Paper presented at Western
        Historical Society Meeting,
        1962, Denver. MS, Department
        of Anthropology, University of
        Utah. Salt Lake City.

LISTER, ROBERT H., J. RICHARD AMBLER
and FLORENCE C. LISTER

1960   The Coombs Site, Part II. Uni-
        versity of Utah Anthropologi-
        cal Papers, No. 41, Glen Can-
        yon Series, No. 8. Salt Lake
        City.

LISTER, ROBERT H., and HERBERT W. DICK

1952   Archaeology of the Glade Park
        Area--a Progress Report.
        Southwestern Lore, Vol. 17,
        pp. 69-92. Boulder.

LISTER, ROBERT H., and FLORENCE C.
LISTER

1961   The Coombs Site, Part III:
        Summary and Conclusions. Uni-
        versity of Utah Anthropological
        Papers, No. 41, Glen Canyon
        Series, No. 8. Salt Lake City.

LOHR, EDISON P.

1948   Winter Dig in Yampa Canyon.
        Desert Magazine, Vol. 11,
        No. 6, pp. 9-11. El Centro.

LONG, PAUL V., JR.

1965*   Archaeological Excavations in
        Glen Canyon, Utah-Arizona,
        1959-1960. MA thesis, Depart-
        ment of Anthropology, Univer-
        sity of Arizona. Tucson. Also,
        Museum of Northern Arizona

Bulletin, No. 42, Glen Canyon
Series, No. 7 (1966).
Flagstaff.

LONG, PAUL V., JR., CHRISTY G. TURNER II
and ALEXANDER J. LINDSAY, JR.

1963*   Excavations in Lower Glen Can-
        yon, Utah, 1959-1960. Museum
        of Northern Arizona Bulletin,
        No. 40, Glen Canyon Series,
        No. 6. Flagstaff.

LOSEE, LEONARD, and WILLIAM A. LUCIUS

1975   Archeological Investigations
        in the Maze District, Canyon-
        lands National Park, Utah; and
        Documentation (2 vols.). MS,
        Department of Anthropology,
        University of Utah. Salt Lake
        City.

LOUTHAN, BRUCE D., and DALE L. BERGE

1975*   Archaeological Survey of the
        Huntington-Sigurd Transmission
        Line of Bureau of Land Manage-
        ment Lands. Report to Utah
        Power and Light. MS, Depart-
        ment of Anthropology, Brigham
        Young University. Provo.

LUCIUS, WILLIAM A. (ed.)

1976   Archeological Investigations
        in the Maze District, Canyon-
        lands National Park, Utah.
        Antiquities Section Selected
        Papers, Vol. 3, No. 11. Utah
        State Historical Society,
        Salt Lake City.

LUCIUS, WILLIAM A., and JEFFREY COLVILLE

1976   Osteological Analysis of
        Faunal Remains. In "Sudden
        Shelter," Jesse D. Jennings,
        Alan R. Schroedl and Richard N.
        Holmer. University of Utah
        Anthropological Papers, in
        press. Salt Lake City.

LYMAN, ALBERT R.

1909   The Land of Pagahrit. Improvement Era, Vol. 12, No. 12, pp. 934-38. Salt Lake City.

MCCANDLESS, L.S.

1921*   Explorations in Castle Park, Colorado. Steamboat Pilot.

MCGREGOR, JOHN C.

1941   Southwestern Archaeology. John Wiley & Sons, New York.

1965   Southwestern Archaeology. 2d edition. University of Illinois Press, Urbana.

MCKUSICK, MARSHALL

1960*   Expedition Report, 1960 Archaeological Field School, U.C.L.A. MS, Department of Anthropology, University of California at Los Angeles. Los Angeles.

1961   Puebloid Cultures in Iron County: Progress Report. Utah Archeology, Vol. 7, No. 2, pp. 19-23. Salt Lake City.

MACLEOD, R. BRUCE

1959   Supplemental Report of Robert D. Stirland's Reconnaissance in the Jones Hole Area. MS, Dinosaur National Monument Headquarters. Jensen.

MCLOYD, CHARLES, and C.C. GRAHAM

1894*   Catalogue and Description of a Very Large Collection of Prehistoric Relics Obtained in the Cliff Houses and Caves of Southeastern Utah. MS, Harvard University. Cambridge.

MCNITT, FRANK

1957   Richard Wetherill: Anasazi. University of New Mexico Press, Albuquerque.

MACOMB, J.N.

1876*   Report of the Exploring Expedition from Santa Fe, New Mexico, to the Junction of the Grand and Green Rivers of the Great Colorado of the West in 1859. Washington, D.C.

MADSEN, DAVID B.

1970   Median Village Ceramics and the Distribution of Fremont Plain Gray Ware. In "Median Village and Fremont Culture Regional Vairation," John P. Marwitt. University of Utah Anthropological Papers, No. 95, pp. 54-74. Salt Lake City.

1971a American Telephone and Telegraph Survey. MS, Department of Anthropology, University of Utah. Salt Lake City.

1971b O'Malley Shelter. MA thesis, Department of Anthropology, University of Utah. Salt Lake City.

1973* The Pollen Analysis of O'Malley Shelter. In "Prehistory of Southeastern Nevada," Don D. Fowler, et al. Desert Research Institute Publications in the Social Sciences, No. 6. Reno.

1974   Excavations: Sandy, Utah. Utah Archeology, Vol. 20, No. 2, p. 4. Salt Lake City.

1975a Dating Paiute-Shoshoni Expansion in the Great Basin. American Antiquity, Vol. 40, No. 1, pp. 82-86. Washington, D.C.

1975b Three Fremont Sites in Emery County, Utah. Antiquities Section Selected Papers, Vol. 1, No. 1. Utah State Historical Society, Salt Lake City.

1976a Pint-Size Shelter and the Question of an Archaic/Fremont Hiatus. Paper presented at the Great Basin Anthropological Conference, 1976, Las Vegas.

1976b   Bulldozer Dune (42S146). _Antiquities Section Selected Papers_, Vol. 2, No. 6. Utah State Historical Society, Salt Lake City.

1977   _Pollen Analysis at Agricultural Village Sites: a Test Case at Backhoe Village_. Paper presented at Society for American Archaeology Meeting, 1977, New Orleans.

n.d.   Great Salt Lake Fremont Ceramics. _In_ "The Levee and Knoll Sites," Gary F. Fry, and Gardiner F. Dalley. _University of Utah Anthropological Papers_, in press. Salt Lake City.

MADSEN, DAVID B., and MICHAEL S. BERRY

1973   _Utah Archeological Survey_. MS, Midwest Archeological Center. Lincoln.

1974   _Box Elder County Summary_. MS, Antiquities Section, Utah State Historical Society. Salt Lake City.

1975   A Reassessment of Northeastern Great Basin Prehistory. _American Antiquity_, Vol. 40, No. 4, pp. 391-405. Washington, D.C.

MADSEN, DAVID B., and LAMAR W. LINDSAY

1977   Backhoe Village. _Antiquities Section Selected Papers_, Vol. 4, No. 12. Utah State Historical Society, Salt Lake City.

MADSEN, REX

1972   Evans Mound Ceramics. _In_ "The Evans Site," Michael S. Berry. _A Special Report_, pp. 45-96. Department of Anthropology, University of Utah. Salt Lake City.

1973a   _Fremont Ceramic Types_. MS, Department of Anthropology, University of Utah. Salt Lake City.

1973b   Ceramics from the U-95 Sites. _In_ "Highway U-95 Archeology: Comb Wash to Grand Flat," Gardiner F. Dalley (ed.). _A Special Report_, pp. 222-39. Department of Anthropology, University of Utah. Salt Lake City.

1975   _Topography, Climate, and Soil Types as Indicators of Fremont Regional Variation_. MS, Department of Anthropology, University of Utah. Salt Lake City.

1977   Prehistoric Ceramics of the Fremont. _Museum of Northern Arizona Ceramic Series_, No. 6. Flagstaff.

MAGUIRE, DON

1899   _Antiquities of the Southwest_. Historical Society of Utah, 2d Annual Meeting.

MALDE, HAROLD E., and ASHER P. SCHICK

1964   Geology: Thorne Cave, Northeastern Utah. _American Antiquity_, Vol. 30, No. 1, pp. 60-73. Washington, D.C.

MALLERY, GARRICK

1886   Pictographs of the North American Indians: a Preliminary Paper. _Bureau of American Ethnology Annual Report_, No. 4, pp. 1882-83. Washington, D.C.

1893   Picture-Writing of the American Indians. _Bureau of American Ethnology Annual Report_, No. 10, pp. 1888-89. Washington, D.C.

MALOUF, CARLING

1939   Prehistoric Exchange in Utah. _University of Utah Archeology and Ethnology Papers_, No. 1. Also, _University of Utah Anthropological Papers_, No. 1 (1950). Salt Lake City.

1940a   Prehistoric Exchange in the Northern Periphery of the Southwest. American Antiquity, Vol. 6, No. 2, pp. 115-22. Washington, D.C.

1940b   The Goshiute Indians. University of Utah Archeology and Ethnology Papers, No. 3. Salt Lake City.

1941*   Notes on the Archeology of the Barrier Canyon Region, Utah. The Masterkey, Vol. 15, No. 4, pp. 150-53. Los Angeles.

1944   Thoughts on Utah Archeology. American Antiquity, Vol. 9, pp. 319-28. Washington, D.C.

1946   The Deep Creek Region, the Northwestern Frontier of the Pueblo Culture. American Antiquity, Vol. 12, pp. 117-21. Washington, D.C.

MALOUF, CARLING, CHARLES E. DIBBLE and ELMER R. SMITH

1940   The Archeology of the Deep Creek Region. University of Utah Archeology and Ethnology Papers, No. 5. Also, University of Utah Anthropological Papers, No. 5 (1950). Salt Lake City.

MARTIN, PAUL S.

1964   Pollen Analysis in the Glen Canyon. In "1962 Excavations, Glen Canyon Area," Floyd W. Sharrock, et al. University of Utah Anthropological Papers, No. 73, Glen Canyon Series, No. 25, pp. 176-95. Salt Lake City.

MARTIN, PAUL S., and FLOYD W. SHARROCK

1964   Pollen Analysis of Prehistoric Human Feces: a New Approach to Ethnobotany. American Antiquity, Vol. 30, No. 2, pp. 168-80. Washington, D.C. Also,

University of Arizona Contribution, No. 86, Program in Geochronology. Tucson.

MARWITT, JOHN P.

1966   Preliminary Survey of the Monticello Ranger District, Manti LaSal National Forest Survey, Southwest Utah. MS, Department of Anthropology, University of Utah. Also, University of Utah Anthropological Papers, No. 89, Miscellaneous Collected Papers, No. 16 (1967). Salt Lake City.

1968   Pharo Village. University of Utah Anthropological Papers, No. 91. Salt Lake City.

1969a   Prehistoric Man in Utah: a Summary. In Guidebook tc Northern Utah, D. Gray (ed.), pp. 21-35. Utah Geological Survey, Salt Lake City.

1969b   Preliminary Report of Excavations at Median Village, Summit, Iron County, Utah. MS, Department of Anthropology, University of Utah. Salt Lake City.

1970a   Archeological Inspection of Proposed Road from Squaw Flats to Confluence Overlook, Canyonlands National Park, Utah. MS, National Park Service Western Service Center. Santa Fe.

1970b   Parowan Fremont. Paper presented at the Fremont Culture Symposium, Society for American Archaeology Meeting, 1970, Mexico City. MS, Department of Anthropology, University of Utah. Salt Lake City.

1970c   Median Village and Fremont Culture Regional Variation. University of Utah Anthropological Papers, No. 95. Salt Lake City.

MARWITT, JOHN P., and GARY F. FRY

1973   Radiocarbon Dates from Utah. Southwestern Lore, Vol. 38, pp. 1–9. Boulder.

MARWITT, JOHN P., GARY F. FRY and JAMES M. ADOVASIO

1971*   Sandwich Shelter. In "Great Basin Anthropological Conference 1970 Selected Papers," C. Melvin Aikens (ed.). University of Oregon Anthropological Papers, No. 1. Eugene.

MATHENY, RAY T.

1962*   An Archaeological Survey of Upper Montezuma Canyon, San Juan County, Utah. MA thesis, Department of Anthropology, Brigham Young University. Provo.

1967*   Annual Report for Archaeological Field Work, Brigham Young University. MS, Department of Anthropology, Brigham Young University. Provo.

1971*   Archaeological Survey of Huntington Canyon Salvage Project, June 1971. Report to Utah Power and Light. MS, Department of Anthropology, Brigham Young University. Provo.

1975*   Cultural Developments in the Central Colorado Plateau; Archaeological Survey of the Pinto-Abajo Transmission Line, Southeastern Utah. A Special Report. Department of Anthropology, Brigham Young University. Provo.

n.d.a*   Preliminary Report, Brigham Young University, Field School of Archaeology, 1969-71. MS, Department of Anthropology, Brigham Young Univeristy. Provo.

n.d.b.   Clay Hills Archeology Salvage. MS, Department of Anthropology, University of Utah. Salt Lake City.

(ED.)

1974   The Elk Ridge Archaeological Project, Manti-LaSal National Forest: Summary of the 1972 Season. MS, Department of Anthropology, Brigham Young University. Provo.

MATHEWS, THOMAS W.

1957   Descriptive Analysis of Pottery for the 1957 Season: Upper Colorado River Basin Archeological Salvage Project. MS, Department of Anthropology, University of Utah. Salt Lake City.

1958   Grand Gulch Survey. MS, Department of Anthropology, University of Utah. Salt Lake City.

MAYNARD, C.C.

1911   Hieroglyphics near Benjamin, Utah. Improvement Era, Vol. 14, No. 6, pp. 582-90. Salt Lake City.

MEIGHAN, CLEMENT

1955   Excavation at Paragonah, Utah. Utah Archeology, Vol. 1, No. 3, p. 4. Salt Lake city.

1968   Review of Aikens, "Virgin-Kayenta Cultural Relationships"; Cutler, "Corn, Cucurbits and Cotton from Glen Canyon"; Jennings, "Glen Canyon: a Summary"; and Long, "Archeological Excavations

vations in Lower Glen Canyon, 1959-1960." American Anthropologist, Vol. 70, No. 1. Washington, D.C.

MEIGHAN, CLEMENT W., et al.

1956   Archeological Excavations in Iron County, Utah. University of Utah Anthropological Papers, No. 25. Salt Lake City.

MILLER, BLAINE A.

1976   Study of a Prudden Unit Site (42Sa-971-N) in Montezuma Canyon, San Juan County, Utah. MA thesis, Department of Anthropology, Brigham Young University. Provo.

MILLER, DAVID E.

1958   Discovery of Glen Canyon, 1776. Utah Historical Quarterly, Vol. 26, No. 3, pp. 220-37. Salt Lake City.

MILLER, DONALD E.

1974   A Synthesis of Excavations at Site 42SaB63, Three Kiva Pueblo, Montezuma Canyon, San Juan County, Utah. MA thesis, Department of Anthropology, Brigham Young University. Provo.

MILLER, WADE

n.d.*   Late Pleistocene Vertebrates of the Silver Creek Local Fauna from North-central Utah. Journal of Paleontology, in press. Lawrence.

MILLER, WICK R.

1966*   Anthropological Linguistics in the Great Basin. In "Current Status of Anthropological Research in the Great Basin: 1964," W.L. d'Azevedo, et al. (eds.). Desert Research Publications in the Social Sciences, No. 1, pp. 75-112. Reno.

1970   Western Shoshoni Dialects. In Languages and Cultures of Western North American, Essays in Honor of Sven S. Liljeblad, Earl H. Swanson, Jr. (ed.), pp. 17-36. Idaho State University Press, Pocatello.

1972   Newe Natekwinappeh: Shoshoni Stories and Dictionary. University of Utah Anthropological Papers, No. 94. Salt Lake City.

MILLER, WICK R., JAMES TANNER and LAWRENCE FOLEY

1969   A Lexicostatistic Study of Shoshoni Dialects. Anthropological Linguistics, Vol. 13, No. 4, pp. 142-164. Bloomington.

MILLER, WILLIAM C., and DAVID A. BRETERNITZ

1958a   1957 Navajo Canyon Survey -- Preliminary Report. Plateau, Vol. 30, No. 3, pp. 72-74. Flagstaff.

1958b   1958 Navajo Canyon Survey -- Preliminary Report. Plateau, Vol. 31, No. 1, pp. 3-7. Flagstaff.

MOCK, JAMES M.

1969*   Radiocarbon Dates from Spotten Cave, Utah. MS, Department of Anthropology, Brigham Young University. Provo.

1971*   The Archeology of Spotten Cave, Utah County, Central Utah. MA thesis, Department of Anthropology, Brigham Young University. Provo.

MOFFITT, KATHLEEN, SANDRA RAYL and MICHAEL METCALF

1975*   Archaeological Investigations of 62 Prehistoric Sites Along the Navajo-McCullough Transmission Line, Southern Utah and Northern Arizona. MS, Museum of Northern Arizona. Flagstaff.

MOHR, ALBERT, and L.L. SAMPLE

1959   San Jose Sites in Southeastern Utah. El Palacio, Vol. 66, pp. 109-119. Santa Fe.

MONTGOMERY, HENRY

1894* Prehistoric Man in Utah. The Archaeologist, Vol. 2, No. 8, pp. 227-34; No. 10, pp. 298-306; No. 11, pp. 335-42. Waterloo.

MONTILLO, ERLINDA D.

1968   A Study of the Prehistoric Settlement Patterns of the Provo Area in Central Utah. MA thesis, Department of Anthropology, Brigham Young University. Provo.

MOORE, JOHN G., GARY F. FRY, and E. ENGLERT, JR.

1969   Thorny-Headed Worm Infection in North American Prehistoric Man. Science, Vol. 163, pp. 1324-325. Washington, D.C.

MORRIS, EARL H.

1922   An Unexplored Area of the Southwest. Natural History, Vol. 22, No. 6, pp. 498-515. New York.

1929* A Brief Summary of Archaeological Observations Made Along the Route of the Seventh Bernheimer Expedition, 1929. MS, Department of Anthropology, University of Colorado. Boulder.

MORRIS, EARL H., and R.F. BURGH

1941* Anasazi Basketry, Basketmaker II Through Pueblo III: a Study Based on Specimens from the San Juan River Country. Carnegie Institution of Washington Publications, No. 533. Washington, D.C.

MORRIS, RICHARD, et al.

1937* The Canyon of Lodore-Yampa River Reconnaissance of 1936. Trail and Timberline, Vol. 219, pp. 3-14. Denver.

MORRISON, R.B.

1965   New Evidence on Lake Bonneville Stratigraphy and History from Southern Promontory Point, Utah. U.S. Geological Survey Professional Papers, No. 525-C. Washington, D.C. Also, Utah Archeology, Vol. 21, No. 1, pp. 9-20. Salt Lake City.

MORSS, NOEL

1931   The Ancient Culture of the Fremont River in Utah. Peabody Museum of American Archaeology and Ethnology, Harvard University, Papers, Vol. 12, No. 3. Cambridge.

1954   Clay Figurines of the American Southwest, with a Description of the New Pillings Find in Northeastern Utah and a Comparison with Certain Other North American Figurines. Peabody Museum of American Archaeology and Ethnology, Harvard University, Papers, Vol. 49, No. 1. Cambridge.

1957   Appendix I: Figurines. In "Two Fremont Sites and Their Position in Southwestern Prehistory," Dee C. Taylor. University of Utah Anthropological Papers, No. 29, pp. 167-70. Salt Lake City.

MOSELEY, M. EDWARD

1966   The Discovery and Definition
        of Basketmaker: 1890 to 1914.
        The Masterkey, Vol. 40, No. 4,
        pp. 140-54. Los Angeles.

MULROY, MARY E.

1961   Ceramic Distribution in South-
        eastern Utah. MS, Department
        of Anthropology, University
        of Utah. Salt Lake City.

MULROY, MARY E., and MAKOTO KOWTA

1964   An Archeological Survey of
        Capitol Reef National Monu-
        ment. MS, Department of
        Anthropology, University of
        Utah. Salt Lake City.

MURBARGER, NELL

1960   First Pack Train Over the Tava-
        puts. Desert Magazine, Vol. 23,
        No. 3, pp. 24-27 and 34.
        El Centro.

NEELY, JAMES, and ALAN P. OLSON

1963*   A Survey of Monument Valley,
        Northeastern Arizona. MS,
        Museum of Northern Arizona.
        Flagstaff.

1965*   A Report to the Navajo Tribe
        on the Archaeological Poten-
        tial of Monument Valley Tribal
        Park. MS, Museum of Northern
        Arizona. Flagstaff.

NEWBERRY, J.S.

1876   Geological Report. In Report
        of the Exploring Expedition
        from Santa Fe, New Mexico, to
        the Junction of the Grand and
        Green Rivers of the Great
        Colorado of the West, in 1859,
        J.N. Macomb. U.S. Engineering
        Department, Washington, D.C.

NICHOLS, JAMES L.

1958   A Preliminary Report of the
        Roving Survey of the West Bank
        of the Colorado River, Behind
        the Area to be Inundated by the
        Glen Canyon Project. MS, Depart-
        ment of Anthropology, Univer-
        sity of Utah. Salt Lake City.

NIELSON, ASA S.

1976*   A Preliminary Report on the
        Archaeological Survey of the
        Sigurd-Cedar City Transmission
        Line. A Special Report,
        Department of Anthropology,
        Brigham Young University. Provo.

NIELSON, GLENNA

1975*   Archaeological Survey of the
        Huntington-Sigurd Transmission
        Line Over the Fish Lake Nation-
        al Forest. Report to Utah
        Power and Light. MS, Department
        of Anthropology, Brigham Young
        University. Provo.

NUSBAUM, JESSE L.

1922*   A Basket-Maker Cave in Kane
        County, Utah; with Notes on
        the Artifacts by A.V. Kidder
        and S.J. Guernsey. Museum of
        the American Indian, Heye
        Foundation, Indian Notes and
        Monographs, Miscellaneous,
        No. 29. New York.

O'NEILL, FLOYD A.

1973*   A History of the Ute Indians
        of Utah Until 1890. Ph.D.
        dissertation, University of
        Utah. Salt Lake City.

OPLER, M.K.

1939*   Southern Ute Pottery Types.
        The Masterkey, Vol. 13, pp.
        161-63. Los Angeles.

1943   The Origins of Comanche and
        Ute. American Anthropolgist,
        Vol. 45, pp. 155-58. Washing-
        ton, D.C.

OSBORNE, D.

1941* Archaeological Reconnaissance
in Western Utah and Nevada,
1939. The Masterkey, Vol. 15,
No. 5, pp. 189-95. Los Angeles.

PALMER, E.

1876 Exploration of a Mound in Utah.
American Naturalist, Vol. 10,
pp. 410-14. Cambridge.

1878 Cave Dwellings in Utah.
Peabody Museum of American
Archaeology and Ethnology,
Harvard University, Eleventh
Annual Report, Vol. 2, No. 2,
pp. 269-72. Cambridge.

PATTERSON, GREGORY R.

1975 A Preliminary Study of an
Anasazi Settlement (42Sa971)
Prior to A.D. 900 in Monte-
zuma Canyon, San Juan County,
Southeastern Utah. MA thesis,
Department of Anthropology,
Brigham Young University.
Provo.

PENDERGAST, DAVID M.

1960 Archeological Resources of
Fish Springs National Wildlife
Refuge: Preliminary Report.
MS, Department of Anthropology,
University of Utah. Salt Lake
City.

1961a Excavations at the Bear River
Site, Box Elder County, Utah.
Utah Archeology, Vol. 7, No.
2, pp. 14-18. Salt Lake City.

1961b USAS-UCRBASP Joint Excavation
in the Plainfield Reservoir.
Utah Archeology, Vol. 7, No.
3, pp. 15-21. Salt Lake City.

1961c 1960 Test Excavations in the
Plainfield Reservoir Area. In
"1960 Excavations, Glen Canyon Area," Floyd W. Sharrock,
et al. University of Utah
Anthropological Papers, No.
52. Salt Lake City.

1962 The Frei Site, Santa Clara,
Utah. In "Miscellaneous Collected Papers," James H. Gunnerson, David M. Pendergast,
and Keith M. Anderson. University of Utah Anthropological
Papers, No. 60, pp. 127-63.
Salt Lake City.

1963 Lithic Materials from South-
western Wyoming and North-
eastern Utah. In "Archeological
Survey of the Flaming Gorge
Reservoir Area, Wyoming-Utah,"
Kent C. Day and David S.
Dibble. University of Utah
Anthropological Papers, No. 65,
Upper Colorado Series, No. 9.
Salt Lake City.

PENDERGAST, DAVID M., and FRANCIS K.
HASSEL

1962 A Burial from an Open Site in
Willard Reservoir, Box Elder
County, Utah. Utah Archeology,
Vol. 8, No. 1, pp. 22-24.

PEPPER, GEORGE H.

1902 The Ancient Basket Makers of
Southeastern Utah. American
Museum of Natural History
Journal, Supplement, Vol. 2,
No. 4. New York.

PERRINS, GLEN

1929 The Indians--Yesterday and Today. Improvement Era, Vol. 32,
pp. 386-90. Salt Lake City.

PETERSON, H. MERRILL

1963 History and Pre-History of
Bear Lake Indians. Utah
Archeology, Vol. 9, No. 4,
pp. 3-8. Salt Lake City.

1964 Indian Cache Uncovered. Utah
Archeology, Vol. 10, No. 4,
pp. 2-3. Salt Lake City.

PETERSON, KENNETH LEE

1969   A New Variant of the Fremont Moccasin. Utah Archeology, Vol. 15, No. 1, pp. 4-9. Salt Lake City.

PIERSON, LLOYD

1957   A Brief Archeological Reconnaissance of White Canyon, Southeastern Utah. El Palacio, Vol. 64, Nos. 7-8, pp. 222-30. Santa Fe.

1958   An Undercut Storage Pit Near Moab, Utah. Utah Archeology, Vol. 4, No. 1, pp. 4-6. Salt Lake City.

1959   Archeological Resources of the Beef Basin, Needles, Salt Creek Area. MS, Department of Anthropology, University of Utah. Salt Lake City.

1960   Ute Tipi Poles. Utah Archeology, Vol. 6, No. 4, pp. 10-12. Salt Lake City.

1962   Archeological Resources of the Needles-Salt Creek Area, Utah. Utah Archeology, Vol. 8, No. 2, pp. 1-3. Salt Lake City.

n.d.*   Archeological Reports. MS, Arches National Park.

PIERSON, LLOYD, and KEVIN ANDERSON

1975   Another Split-Twig Figurine from Moab, Utah. Plateau, Vol. 48, Nos. 1-2, pp. 43-45. Flagstaff.

POWELL, JOHN W.

1870   Major J.W. Powell's Report on his Explorations of the Rio Colorado in 1869. Utah Historical Quarterly, Vol. 15, pp. 21-27 (1947). Salt Lake City.

1875   Explorations of the Colorado River of the West and its Tributaries. Explored in 1869, 1870, 1871, and 1872, Under the Direction of the Secretary of the Smithsonian Institution. Government Printing Office, Washington, D.C.

PRICE, SARA SUE

1952   A Comparison of Gosiute Material Culture and the Archeology of Western Utah. MA thesis, Department of Anthropology, University of Utah. Salt Lake City.

PRUDDEN, T. MITCHELL

1897   An Elder Brother to the Cliff-Dweller. Harper's New Monthly Magazine, Vol. 95, pp. 56-62. New York.

1903   The Prehistoric Ruins of the San Juan Watershed in Utah, Arizona, Colorado, and New Mexico. American Anthropologist, Vol. 5, No. 2, pp. 224-88. Washington, D.C.

1914   The Circular Kivas of Small Ruins in the San Juan Watershed. American Anthropologist, Vol. 16, No. 1, pp. 33-58. Washington, D.C.

1918   A Further Study of Prehistoric Small House Ruins in the San Juan Watershed. American Anthropological Association Memoirs, Vol. 5, No. 1, pp. 3-50. Washington, D.C.

PUTNAM, F.W.

1876   Reports of the Peabody Museum, Harvard University, Vol. I (1868-1876). Cambridge.

1880   Reports of the Peabody Museum, Harvard University, Vol. II (1876-1879). Cambridge.

PUTNAM, J.D.

1876   Hieroglyphics Observed in
Summit Canyon, Utah and on
Little Popo-agie River in Wyo-
ming. Davenport Academy of
Natural Sciences Proceedings,
1867-1876, Vol. 1, pp. 143-45.

PURDY, WILLIAM M.

1959a   Appendix I: Final Report;
Preliminary Survey of the
Flaming Gorge Reservoir, 1958.
In "An Outline of the History
of the Flaming Gorge Area,"
William M. Purdy. University
of Utah Anthropological Papers,
No. 37, Upper Colorado Series,
No. 1, pp. 37-39. Salt Lake
City.

1959b   An Outline of the History of
the Flaming Gorge Area. University of Utah Anthropological Papers, No. 37, Upper
Colorado Series, No. 1. Salt
Lake City.

REAGAN, ALBERT B.

1917*   The Deep Creek Indians. El
Palacio, Vol. 4, No. 3, pp.
30-42. Santa Fe.

1931a*   Ancient Writings North of the
Rio Grande. Roger Williams
Naturalist, Vol. 3, No. 4,
pp. 1-6.

1931b   Ruins of Dawning Age Found in
Northeastern Utah. Science
Service, December 8, 1930.
Science Newsletter, January 3,
1931. Washington, D.C.

1931c*   Some Notes on the Picture
Writing North of Mexico.
Wagner Free Institute of Sci-
ence of Philadelphia Bulletin,
Vol. 7, No. 4, pp. 38-54.
Philadelphia.

1931d   Archaeological Finds in the
Uinta Basin, 1931. In
"Archaeological Field Work in

North American During 1931."
Committee on State Archaeolo-
gical Surveys, Reports, p. 41.
Ann Arbor.

1931e   Early House Builders of the
Brush Creek Region in Northeastern Utah. American Anthropologist, Vol. 33, No. 4, pp.
660-61. Washington, D.C.

1931f   The Pictographs in Ashley and
Dry Fork Valleys, in Northeastern Utah. Kansas Academy
of Science Transactions, Vol.
34, pp. 168-216. Topeka.

1931g   Ruins and Pictographs in Nine
Mile Canyon, Utah. Illinois
State Academy of Science Transactions, Vol. 24, No. 2, pp.
369-70. Springfield.

1931h   Some Archaeological Notes on
Nine Mile Canyon, Utah. El
Palacio, Vol. 31, No. 4, pp.
45-71. Santa Fe.

1931i   Collections of Ancient Artifacts from the Ashley-Dry Fork
District of the Uinta Basin,
With Some Notes on the Dwellings and Mortuary Customs of
the Ute Indians of the Ouray
(Utah) Region. El Palacio, Vol.
31, No. 26, pp. 407-413.
Santa Fe.

1931j   Some Archaeological Notes on
Hill Canyon in Northwestern
Utah. El Palacio, Vol. 31, No.
15, pp. 223-44. Santa Fe.

1931k   Some Notes on the Ancient
Earth-Lodge Peoples of the
Willard Stage of Pueblo Culture
in the Uintah Basin, Utah.
El Palacio, Vol. 30, Nos. 19-
20. Santa Fe.

1931L   Addition Archaeological Notes
on Ashley and Dry Fork Canyons
in Northeastern Utah. El Palacio, Vol. 31, No. 8, pp. 122-
31. Santa Fe.

1931m* Nine Mile Canyon, A Review. _Discoveries_, Vol. 2, No. 2, p. 8.

1931n* Rock Writings in Utah. _Discoveries_, Vol. 2, No. 3, p.6.

1931o* Archeological Notes on the Brush Creek Region, Northeastern Utah. _The Wisconsin Archeologist_, Vol. 10, No. 4, pp. 132-38. Milwaukee.

1931p Caves of the Vernal District of Northeastern Utah (Abstract). _Utah Academy of Sciences, Arts and Letters Proceedings_, Vol. 10, pp. 13-18. Salt Lake City.

1931q Indian Pictures in Ashley and Dry Fork Valleys, in Northeastern Utah. _Art and Archaeology_, Vol. 34, No. 4, pp. 200-205, 210. Washington, D.C.

1932a The Ancient House People of the Brush Creek Region, in Northeastern Utah. _Iowa Academy of Science Proceedings for 1931_, pp. 183-84. Des Moines.

1932b* Archaeological Finds in the Uinta Basin in Utah. _The Wisconsin Archaeologist_, Vol. 11, pp. 162-71. Milwaukee.

1932c Archaeological Finds in Northeastern Utah. _Iowa Academy of Science Proceedings_, Vol. 40, pp. 131-32. Des Moines.

1932d* The Ancient Agriculturalists of Brush Creek Valley, in Northeastern Utah. _Frontiers_, Vol. 12, No. 2, pp. 174-76. Philadelphia.

1932e Finds in the Uintah Basin, in Utah, in 1931. _American Anthropologist_, Vol. 34, No. 3, p. 505. Washington, D.C.

1933a Anciently Inhabited Caves of the Vernal (Utah) District with Some Additional Notes on Nine Mile Canyon, Northeast Utah. _Kansas Academy of Sciences Transactions_, Vol. 36, pp. 41-70. Topeka.

1933b The Basket Makers and the People of the Ancient Culture of the Fremont River in Utah. _Northwest Science_, Vol. 8, No. 3. Pullman.

1933c Some Notes on the Snake Pictographs of Nine Mile Canyon, Utah. _American Anthropologist_, Vol. 35, No. 3, p. 550. Washington, D.C.

1933d Evidence of Migration in Ancient Pueblo Times. _American Anthropologist_, Vol. 35, No. 1, pp. 206-207. Washington, D.C.

1933e Report of Archaeological Field Work During 1932. _American Anthropologist_, Vol. 35, No. 3, p. 508. Washington, D.C.

1933f Summary of Archeological Finds in the Uintah Basin, in Utah, to date. _Utah Academy of Science, Arts and Letters_, Vol. 10, pp. 3-18. Salt Lake City.

1934a* Evidence of Possible Migration in the Very Dawning Period of Pueblo Culture. _Primitive Man_, Vol. 7, pp. 12-14. Washington, D.C.

1934b Some Ancient Indian Granaries. _Utah Academy of Science, Arts and Letters_, Vol. 11, pp. 39-42. Salt Lake City.

1934c Some Notes on the History of the Uinta Basin in Northeastern Utah, to 1850. _Utah Academy of Science, Arts and Letters_, Vol. 11, pp. 55-64. Salt Lake City.

1934d* Additional Archaeological Notes on the Uintah Basin, in Northeastern Utah. _Kansas Academy of Science Transactions_, Vol. 37, pp. 39-54. Topeka.

1934e* Archaeological Field Work in Utah. Archaeological Field Work in North America in 1933. Circular Series 18, pp. 40-41.

1935a Archeological Report of Field Work Done in Utah in 1934-35. Utah Academy of Science, Arts and Letters, Vol. 12, pp. 50-88. Salt Lake City.

1935b Petroglyphs Show that the Ancients of the Southwest Wore Masks. American Anthropologist, Vol. 37, pp. 707-708. Washington, D.C.

1935c Two Rock Pictures and Their Probable Connection with the "Pied Piper" Myth of the Indians. The Colorado Magazine, Vol. 12, No. 2, pp. 55-59. Denver.

1935d* An Archeological Trip to Buck Horn Draw - Indians Worshipping the Sun. Utah Academy of Sciences, Arts and Letters, Vol. 12. Salt Lake City.

1935e* Trip to Bull Hollow Wash, May 3-4, 1935. Utah Academy of Sciences, Arts and Letters, Vol. 12. Salt Lake City.

1937a Ancient Utah People Seem to Have Believed that Snakes Evolved from an Animal. The Wisconsin Archaeologist, Vol. 15, No. 2, p. 44. Milwaukee.

1937b Investigations of the Uintah Basin and Pueblo II Type Culture in the Uintah Basin, Mentioned. Summary of Archaeological Work in the Two Americas. Archaeological Series, No. 7, p. 59.

1937c Discoveries of Brigham Young University Archaeological Party Regarding Ancient Fremont Peoples. Science Service, Science Newsletter, July 13, 1937.

REED, ERIK K.

1946 The Distinctive Features and Distribution of the San Juan Anasazi Culture. Southwestern Journal of Anthropology, Vol. 2, No. 3, pp. 295-305. Albuquerque.

1955 Human Skeletal Remains from the Turner-Look Site. In "A Reappraisal of the Fremont Culture," H.M. Wormington. Denver Museum of Natural History Proceedings, No. 1, pp. 38-43. Denver.

1963a Appendix III: Human Skeletal Material from Moqui Canyon, Southeastern Utah. In "1961 Excavations, Glen Canyon Area," Floyd W. Sharrock, Kent C. Day and David S. Dibble. University of Utah Anthropological Papers, No. 63, Glen Canyon Series, No. 18, pp. 307-346. Salt Lake City.

1963b* The Period Known as Pueblo I. Regional Research Abstract, No. 304. National Park Service, Santa Fe.

1964a Appendix III: Human Skeletal Material, 1962 Excavations, Glen Canyon Area. In "1962 Excavations, Glen Canyon Area," Floyd W. Sharrock, et al. University of Utah Anthropological Papers, No. 73, Glen Canyon Series, No. 25, pp. 157-63. Salt Lake City.

1964b The Greater Southwest. In Prehistoric Man in the New World, Jesse D. Jennings, and Edward Norbeck (eds.), pp. 175-92. Rice University Semicentennial Publications, University of Chicago Press, Chicago.

1966a Two Male Crania from the Injun Creek Site, Warren, Utah. MS, Department of Anthropology, University of Utah. Salt Lake City.

1966b Skeletons from the Injun Creek Site. In "Fremont-Promontory-Plains Relationships in Northern Utah," C. Melvin Aikens. University of Utah Anthropological Papers, No. 82, pp.95-101. Salt Lake City.

1966c Human Skeletons from Two Fremont Sites in Utah: A Preliminary Report. In "Caldwell Village," J. Richard Ambler. University of Utah Anthropological Papers, No. 84, pp. 73-91. Salt Lake City.

n.d. La Pointe and Snake Rock Skeletons. MS, Department of Anthropology, University of Utah. Salt Lake City.

REEDER, GRANT

1965 Pictographs from Parrish Canyon, Davis County. Utah Archeology, Vol. 11, No. 3, pp. 5-8. Salt Lake City.

REILEY, DANIEL E.

1969 Two Pueblo II Cradle Burials from Upper Glen Canyon, Utah. MS, Department of Anthropology, University of Utah. Salt Lake City.

RINALDO, JOHN B.

1935* An Archeological Reconnaissance of the San Juan and Colorado Rivers. Rainbow Bridge-Monument Valley Expedition, Preliminary Bulletins, Archeological Series No. 5.

ROBERTS, FRANK H.H., JR.

1935 A Survey of Southwestern Archeology. American Anthropologist, Vol. 37, No. 1, pp. 1-33. Washington, D.C.

1937 Archaeology in the Southwest. American Antiquity, Vol. 3, No. 1, pp. 3-33. Washington, D.C.

ROMNEY, A.K.

1957 The Genetic Model and Uto-Aztecan Time Perspective. Davidson Journal of Anthropology, Vol. 3, pp. 35-41.

ROSS, KENNETH I.

n.d.* Activities of Southwest Explorations in the Salt Creek Area. MS, Canyonlands National Park.

RUBY, JAY, and WAYNE ALEXANDER

1962* Preliminary Report of Excavations at Evans Mound (In-40) Summit, Utah. MS, Department of Anthropology, University of California at Los Angeles. Los Angeles.

RUDY, JACK R.

1952a Archeological Survey Beef Basin-Ruin Park Region, San Juan County. MS, Department of Anthropology, University of Utah. Salt Lake City.

1952b* A Preliminary Accounting of the 1951-52 Research Activities of the Statewide Archeological Survey, Department of Anthropology, University of Utah. Report, Midwest Archeological Center. Lincoln.

1953a* Beef Basin Excavation 1953, Preliminary Statement. Report, Midwest Archeological Center. Lincoln.

1953b An Archeological Survey of Western Utah. University of Utah Anthropological Papers, No. 12. Salt Lake City.

1954a University of Utah Archaeological Field Work, 1952-1953. Southwestern Lore, Vol. 19, No. 4, pp. 13-15. Boulder.

1954b Pine Park Shelter, Washington County, Utah. University of Utah Anthropological Papers, No. 18. Salt Lake City.

1955   Archeological Excavations in Beef Basin, Utah. University of Utah Anthropological Papers, No. 20. Salt Lake City.

RUDY, JACK R, and ROBERT D. STIRLAND

1950   An Archeological Reconnaissance in Washington County, Utah. University of Utah Anthropological Papers, No. 9. Salt Lake City.

RUDY, JACK R., and EARL STODDARD

1954   Site on Fremont Island in Great Salt Lake. American Antiquity, Vol. 19, No. 3, pp. 285-90. Salt Lake City.

RUDY, SARA SUE

1957   Textiles. In "Danger Cave," Jesse D. Jennings. University of Utah Anthropological Papers, No. 27, pp. 235-64. Salt Lake City.

SARGENT, KAY

1977   Emery County: An Archeological Summary. MS, Antiquities Section, Utah State Historical Society. Salt Lake City.

SCHAAFSMA, POLLY

1970   Survey Report of the Rock Art of Utah. MS, Antiquities Section, Utah State Historical Society. Salt Lake City.

1971   The Rock Art of Utah: from the Donald Scott Collection. Peabody Museum of American Archaeology and Ethnology, Harvard University, Papers, Vol. 65. Cambridge.

SCHMITT, KARL

1944   Catalogue of Artifacts from Vicinity of Dugway Proving Grounds, Tooele, Utah. MS, Department of Anthropology, University of Utah. Salt Lake City.

SCHOENWETTER, JAMES

1974*   Palynological Records of Joe's Valley Alcove: A Multicomponent Site in Southeast Utah. A Special Report. Department of Anthropology, Arizona State University. Tempe.

SCHROEDER, ALBERT H.

1954*   Results of Archeological Field Work in Zion National Park, Utah: Based on the 1933-34 C.W.A. Project Supervised by Ben W. Wetherill. Report, National Park Service. Santa Fe.

1955   Archeology of Zion Park. University of Utah Anthropological Papers, No. 22. Salt Lake City.

1956   Book Review, "Pine Park Shelter." El Palacio, Vol. 63, No. 2, pp. 59-61. Santa Fe.

1961   The Archeological Excavations at Willow Beach, Arizona, 1950. University of Utah Anthropological Papers, No. 50. Salt Lake City.

1963   Comment on Gunnerson's "Plateau Shoshonean Prehistory." American Antiquity, Vol. 28, No. 4, pp. 559-60. Washington, D.C.

1964*   Navajo Sites in the National Bridges Area. MS, Natural Bridges National Monument.

1965a   Salvage Excavations at Natural Bridges National Monument. Miscellaneous Papers, No. 10, University of Utah Anthropological Papers, No. 75. Salt Lake City.

1965b   Unregulated Diffusion from Mexico into the Southwest Prior to A.D. 700. American Antiquity Vol. 30, No. 3, pp. 297-309. Washington, D.C.

SCHROEDL, ALAN R.

1974   The Excavation of Innocents
        Ridge. Utah Archeology, Vol.
        20, No. 3, p. 2. Salt Lake
        City.

1975   The Excavation of Cowboy Cave.
        Utah Archeology, Vol. 21, No.
        1, p. 1. Salt Lake City.

1976a   The Bull Creek Excavations.
        Utah Archeology, Vol. 22, No.
        2, pp. 1-4. Salt Lake City.

1976b   Archeological Survey of the
        Dangling Rope Area. MS, De-
        partment of Anthropology,
        University of Utah. Salt Lake
        City.

1976c   The Prehistoric Cultural Re-
        sources of Lake and Moqui Can-
        yons, Glen Canyon National
        Recreation Area. Report, Mid-
        west Archeological Center.
        Lincoln.

1976d   The Archaic of the Northern
        Colorado Plateau. Ph.D. dis-
        sertation, Department of
        Anthropology, University of
        Utah. Salt Lake City.

1976e   Cultural Features. In "Sudden
        Shelter," Jesse D. Jennings,
        Alan R. Schroedl and Richard
        N. Holmer. University of Utah
        Anthropological Papers, in
        press. Salt Lake City.

1976f   Ground Stone, Pottery and Clay.
        In "Sudden Shelter," Jesse D.
        Jennings, Alan R. Schroedl and
        Richard N. Holmer. University
        of Utah Anthropological Papers,
        in press. Salt Lake City.

1977a   The Grand Canyon Figurine Com-
        plex. American Antiquity, Vol.
        42, No. 2, pp. 254-65.
        Washington, D.C.

1977b   The Paleo-Indian Period on the
        Colorado Plateau. Southwestern
        Lore, Vol. 43, in press.
        Boulder.

1978   Archeological Research in Glen
        Canyon, 1977: Report and Recom-
        mendation. Report, Midwest
        Archeological Center. Lincoln.

SCHROEDL, ALAN R., and PATRICK F. HOGAN

1975   Innocents Ridge and the San
        Rafael Fremont. Antiquities
        Section Selected Papers, Vol.
        1, No. 2. Utah State Historical
        Society, Salt Lake City.

SCHULMAN, EDMUND

1948   Dendrochronology in Northeas-
        tern Utah. Tree-Ring Bulletin,
        Vol. 15, Nos. 1, 2. Tucson.

1950   A Dated Beam from Dinosaur
        National Monument. Tree-Ring
        Bulletin, Vol. 16, No. 3, pp.
        18-19. Tucson.

1951   Miscellaneous Ring Records III.
        Tree-Ring Bulletin, Vol. 17,
        No. 4, pp. 28-29. Tucson.

1952   Extension of San Juan Chrono-
        logy to B.C. Times. Tree-Ring
        Bulletin, Vol. 18, No. 4.
        Tucson.

1954   Dendroclimatic Changes in Semi-
        arid Regions. Tree-Ring Bulle-
        tin, Vol. 20, Nos. 3, 4.
        Tucson.

SCHUSTER, CARL

1968*   Incised Stones from Nevada and
        Elswhere. Nevada Archeological
        Survey Reporter, Vol. 2, No. 5,
        pp. 4-23. Reno.

SCOGGIN, CHARLES R.

1941*   Report of Reconnaissance in
        Dinosaur National Monument,
        Season 1941. Report, Dinosaur
        National Monument Headquarters.
        Jensen.

n.d.*   Preliminary Report of the
        Archeological Field Work of the
        University of Colorado Museum
        in Yampa Canyon, Dinosaur NM,

Utah/Colorado. Report, Midwest Archeological Center. Lincoln.

SCOTT, DONALD

1928*   Notes on Reconnaissance of the Kaiparowits Plateau and Adjacent Regions. MS, Department of Anthropology, Harvard University. Cambridge.

SENULIS, JOHN A.

1969   Aboriginal Exploitation Patterns of the Bear River Drainage: 1800-1875. MS, Department of Anthropology, University of Utah. Salt Lake City.

SEVERANCE, MARK S.

1874   Preliminary Ethnological Report. In Progress Report upon Geological and Geographical Explorations and Surveys West of the 100th Meridian, in 1877, G.M. Wheeler. Washington, D.C.

SEVERANCE, MARK S., and H.C. YARROW

1879   Notes upon Human Crania and Skeletons Collected by the Expeditions of 1872-74. United States Geographical Surveys West of the 100th Meridian, Vol. 7. Washington, D.C.

SHARROCK, FLOYD W.

1961a   A Preliminary Report of 1960 Archeological Excavations in Glen Canyon. Utah Archeology, Vol. 7, No. 1, pp. 7-15. Salt Lake City.

1961b   A Preliminary Report of 1961 Archeological Excavations in Moqui Canyon and Castle Wash. Utah Archeology, Vol. 7, No. 4, pp. 6-11. Salt Lake City.

1961c   University of Utah 1961 Field Season. Utah Archeology, Vol. 7, No. 1, p. 24. Salt Lake City.

1961d   University of Utah 1962 Field Season. Utah Archeology, Vol. 7, No. 4, p. 15. Salt Lake City.

1962   A Preliminary Report of 1962 Archeological Excavations in Glen Canyon. Utah Archeology, Vol. 8, No. 4, pp. 1-3. Salt Lake City.

1963   The Hazzard Collection. Archives of Archaeology, No. 23. Society for American Archaeology and the University of Wisconsin Press, Madison.

1966a   An Archeological Survey of Canyonlands National Park. University of Utah Anthropological Papers, No. 83, Miscellaneous Papers, No. 12. Salt Lake City.

1966b   Prehistoric Occupational Patterns in Southwest Wyoming and Cultural Relationships with the Great Basin and Plains Culture Area. University of Utah Anthropological Papers, No. 77. Salt Lake City.

1966c   Preliminary Report on Excavations at the Nephi Site, Nephi, Utah. Utah Archeology, Vol. 12, No. 1, pp. 3-11. Salt Lake City.

1970*   The Sevier Fremont - a Subarea? Paper presented at the Fremont Culture Symposium, Society for American Archaeology Meeting, May 1970, Mexico City.

SHARROCK, FLOYD W., KENT C. DAY and DAVID S. DIBBLE

1963   1961 Excavations, Glen Canyon Area. University of Utah Anthropological Papers, No. 63, Glen Canyon Series, No. 18. Salt Lake City.

SHARROCK, FLOYD W., DAVID S. DIBBLE and
KEITH M. ANDERSON

1961   The Creeping Dune Irrigation
        Site in Glen Canyon, Utah.
        American Antiquity, Vol. 27,
        No. 2, pp. 188-202. Washing-
        ton, D.C.

SHARROCK, FLOYD W., and EDWARD G. KEANE

1962   Carnegie Museum Collection
        from Southeast Utah. University
        of Utah Anthropological Papers,
        No. 57, Glen Canyon Series, No.
        16. Salt Lake City.

SHARROCK, FLOYD W., and JOHN P. MARWITT

1967   Excavations at Nephi, Utah,
        1965-1966. University of Utah
        Anthropological Papers, No.
        88. Salt Lake City.

SHARROCK, FLOYD W., et al.

1961   1960 Excavations, Glen Canyon
        Area. University of Utah An-
        thropological Papers, No. 52,
        Glen Canyon Series, No. 14.
        Salt Lake City.

1964   1962 Excavations, Glen Canyon
        Area. University of Utah An-
        thropological Papers, No. 73,
        Glen Canyon Series, No. 25.
        Salt Lake City.

SHIELDS, WAYNE F.

1967   1966 Excavations: Uinta Basin.
        University of Utah Anthropolo-
        gical Papers, No. 89, Miscel-
        laneous Collected Papers, No.
        15. Salt Lake City.

1968a   The Grantsville Site (42To105):
        1967 Excavations. MS, Depart-
        ment of Anthropology, Univer-
        sity of Utah. Salt Lake City.

1968b   The Historic and Prehistoric
        Cultural Resources of the Up-
        per Colorado River Region. MS,
        Department of Anthropology,
        University of Utah. Salt Lake
        City.

1970*   The Fremont Culture in the
        Uinta Basin. Paper presented
        at the Fremont Culture Sympo-
        sium, Society for American
        Archaeology Meeting, May 1970,
        Mexico City.

n.d.   The Woodruff Bison Kill Site.
        University of Utah Anthropolo-
        gical Papers, Miscellaneous
        Collected Papers, No. 21, in
        press. Salt Lake City.

SHIELDS, WAYNE F., and GARDINER F.
DALLEY

n.d.   The Bear River No. 3 Site.
        University of Utah Anthropolo-
        gical Papers, Miscellaneous
        Collected Papers, No. 22, in
        press. Salt Lake City.

SHIMKIN, DEMITRI B.

1940   Shoshone-Comanche Origins and
        Migrations. Sixth Pacific Sci-
        ence Congress of the Pacific
        Science Association, Proceed-
        ings, Vol. 4, pp. 17-25.
        Berkely.

SIEGRIST, ROLAND (ed.)

1972   Prehistoric Petroglyphs and
        Pictographs in Utah. Utah
        State Historical Society and
        Utah Museum of Fine Arts,
        Salt Lake City.

SISSON, EDWARD B.

1977   Archeological and Historical
        Survey of the Payne Area Near
        the Yellowstone River and of
        the Coyote Basin Area West of
        Neola, Utah. MS, Department of
        Anthropology, University of
        Utah. Salt Lake City.

SISSON, EDWARD B., and CRAIG W. FULLER

1977   Canal Survey of the Uinta
        Basin. MS, Department of
        Anthropology, University of
        Utah. Salt Lake City.

SLEIGHT, FREDERICK W.

1946* Comments on Basketmaker-Like Pictographs in Northern Utah. The Masterkey, Vol. 20, No. 3, pp. 88-92. Los Angeles.

SMITH, ELMER R.

1934 A Brief Description of an Indian Ruin Near Shunesburg, Utah. Zion and Bryce Nature Notes, Vol. 6, pp. 13-18. University of Utah Anthropological Papers, No. 4 (1950). Salt Lake City.

1935 Archeological Resources of Utah. Report to the President of the University of Utah. MS, Department of Anthropology, University of Utah. Salt Lake City.

1936* Utah Type Metates. Bulletin of the Museum of Central Utah, Vol. 1, No. 1.

1937 Archeological Resources of Utah. MS, Department of Anthropology, University of Utah. Salt Lake City.

1938* University of Utah Archaeological Expedition, Summer 1938. Report to the President of the University of Utah. MS, Department of Anthropology, University of Utah. Salt Lake City.

1939* Archaeological Field Work in Utah. The Museum News, Vol. 17, No. 10, p. 3.

1940a* Notes and News. American Antiquities, Vol. 5, No. 4, pp. 344-45.

1940b Areas of Prehistoric and Historical Settlements in Utah. Utah Academy of Science, Arts and Letters Proceedings, Vol. 17, pp. 18-19. Salt Lake City.

1940c PostCaucasion Gosiute Burials from the Deep Creek Area of Utah. Archeology and Ethnology Papers, No. 5. Museum of Anthropology, University of Utah. Also, in "Archeology of the Deep Creek Region," C. Malouf, C.E. Dibble and E. Smith. University of Utah Anthropological Papers, No. 5, pp. 71-75. Salt Lake City.

1941a The Archeology of Deadman Cave, Utah. Bulletin of the University of Utah, Vol. 32, No. 4. Salt Lake City.

1941b An Indian Burial, a Barbed Bone "Projectile Point," and Accompanying Artifacts from Bear Lake, Idaho. Archaeology and Ethnology Papers, No. 6. Museum of Anthropology, University of Utah. Also, University of Utah Anthropological Papers, No. 6. Salt Lake City.

1942* Early Man in the Great Salt Lake Area. Mineralogical Society of Utah News Bulletin, Vol. 13, No. 2, pp. 27-32/

1950 Utah Anthropology. Southwestern Lore, Vol. 16, No. 2, pp. 22-33. Boulder.

1952 The Archeology of Deadman Cave, Utah: A Revision. University of Utah Anthropological Papers, No. 10. Salt Lake City.

SMITH, HOWARD L.

1975* Final Report on Archeological Survey in the Gooseberry Valley. MS, Fish Lake National Forest Supervisor's Office. Richfield.

SMITH, JANET HUGIE

1972 Faunal Remains from the Evans Mound Site. In "The Evans Site," Michael S. Berry. A Special Report. Department of

Anthropology, University of Utah. Salt Lake City.

SMITH, WATSON

n.d.*   Rainbow Bridge Monument Valley Expedition, Utah, 1935. Report, Midwest Archeological Center. Lincoln.

SMITHSONIAN INSTITUTION

1917   Archaeological Reconnaissance in Western Utah. Miscellaneous Collections, Vol. 66, No. 17, pp. 103-108. Washington, D.C.

1918   Archaeological Work in Arizona and Utah. Miscellaneous Collections, Vol. 68, No. 12, pp. 74-83. Washington, D.C.

SNOW, HAROLD L.

1926   Ancient Pictographs of Southern Utah. Improvement Era, Vol. 30, No. 2, pp. 163-65. Salt Lake City.

SPENCER, ALAN C.

1971   An Archeological Survey of the Knolls and Vicinity, Utah County, Utah. MS, Department of Anthropology, University of Utah. Salt Lake City.

SPENCER, JOSEPH E.

1934   Pueblo Sites of Southwestern Utah. American Anthropologist, Vol. 36, No. 1, pp. 70-80. Washington, D.C.

1936   The Middle Virgin Valley, Utah: A Study in Culture Growth and Change. Ph.D. dissertation, University of California. Berkeley.

STALLINGS, W.S.

1941   A Basketmaker II Date from Du Pont Cave, Utah. Tree-Ring Bulletin, Vol. 8, No. 1, pp. 3-6. Tucson.

STANTON, ROBERT B., C. GREGORY CRAMPTON and DWIGHT L. SMITH (eds.)

1961   The Hoskaninni Papers; Mining in Glen Canyon, 1897-1902. University of Utah Anthropological Papers, No. 54, Glen Canyon Series, No. 15. Salt Lake City.

STEELE, DAVID J.

1969   The Determination of Prehistoric Dietary Patterns by Means of Coprolite Analysis: a Glen Canyon Example. Utah Archeology, Vol. 15, No. 2, pp. 3-9. Salt Lake City.

STEEN, CHARLIE R.

1937   Archeological Investigations at Natural Bridges National Monument. Monthly Report, Southwestern Monuments, Vol. 17, pp. 329-337. Santa Fe.

STEWARD, JULIAN H.

1929   Petroglyphs of California and Adjoining States. University of California Publications in American Archaeology and Ethnology, Vol. 24, No. 2. Berkeley.

1931   Archaeological Discoveries at Kanosh in Utah. El Palacio, Vol. 30, No. 8, pp. 121-30. Santa Fe.

1933a* Aborigines of Utah. Utah Resources and Activities, pp. 161-67. Department of Public Instruction.

1933b   Early Inhabitants of Western Utah, Part I - Mounds and House Types. University of Utah Bulletin, Vol. 23, No. 7. Salt Lake City.

1933c   Archaeological Problems of the Northern Periphery of the South West. Museum of Northern Arizona Bulletin, No. 5. Flagstaff.

1936   Pueblo Material Culture in Western Utah. _University of New Mexico Bulletin_, No. 287, _Anthropological Series_, Vol. 1, No. 3. Albuquerque.

1937a   Ancient Caves of the Great Salt Lake Region. _Bureau of American Ethnology Bulletin_, No. 116. Washington, D.C.

1937b   Petroglyphs of the United States. _Smithsonian Institution Annual Report for 1936_, pp. 405-425. Washington, D.C.

1938   Basin-Plateau Aboriginal Sociopolitical Groups. _Bureau of American Ethnology Bulletin_, No. 120. Washington, D.C.

1940   Native Cultures of the Intermontane (Great Basin) Area. _Smithsonian Miscellaneous Collections_, Vol. 100, pp. 445-502. Washington, D.C.

1941a   Archaeological Reconnaissance of Southern Utah. _Bureau of American Ethnology Bulletin_, No. 128, _Anthropological Paper_, No. 18, pp. 277-356. Washington, D.C.

1941b*   Current Element Distributions: XIII, Nevada Shoshone. _University of California Anthropological Records_, Vol. 4, No. 2, pp. 209-359. Berkeley.

1943*   Culture Element Distributions: XXIII, Northern and Gosiute Shoshoni. _University of California Anthropological Records_, Vol. 8, No. 3, pp. 263-392. Berkeley.

1955   Review of Rudy, "Archaeological Survey of Western Utah." _American Antiquity_, Vol. 21, No. 1, pp. 88-89. Washington, D.C.

STIRLAND, ROBERT D.

1947*   _Report on Reconnaissance in Dinosaur National Monument, Jones Hole Area_. MS, Dinosaur National Monument Headquarters. Jensen.

STOKES, WILLIAM LEE and GEORGE H. HANSEN

1941   An Ancient Cave in American Fork Canyon. _Utah Academy of Science, Arts and Letters_, Vol. 18, pp. 27-37. Salt Lake City.

SUHM, DEE ANN

1959a   _Report on Investigations at Two Archeological Sites in the Flaming Gorge Reservoir Area, Daggett County, Utah_. MS, Department of Anthropology, University of Utah. Salt Lake City.

1959b   Extended Survey of the Right Bank of the Glen Canyon. _In_ "The Glen Canyon Archeological Survey, Part I," Don D. Fowler, et al. _University of Utah Anthropological Papers_, No. 39, _Glen Canyon Series_, No. 6. Salt Lake City.

1960a   Additional Artifacts from the 1957 Excavations in the Glen Canyon. _In_ "1959 Excavations, Glen Canyon Area," William D. Lipe, et al. _University of Utah Anthropological Papers_, No. 49, _Glen Canyon Series_, No. 13. Salt Lake City.

1960b   Cataloguing Archeological Collections. _Utah Archeology_, Vol. 6, No. 2, pp. 5-10. Salt Lake City.

SWEENEY, CATHERINE

n.d.   _Ethnohistoric Study in the Glen Canyon_. MS, Department of Anthropology, University of Utah. Salt Lake City.

SWEENEY, CATHERINE, and ROBERT C. EULER

1963*   Southern Paiute Archaeology in
the Glen Canyon Drainage: A
Preliminary Report. Nevada
State Museum Anthropological
Papers, No. 9. Carson City.

TAYLOR, DEE CALDERWOOD

1953   The Garrison Site; A Report
of Archeological Excavations
in Snake Valley, Nevada. MA
thesis, Department of Anthropology, University of Utah.
Salt Lake City.

1954   The Garrison Site. University
of Utah Anthropological Papers,
No. 16. Salt Lake City.

1955   Archeological Excavations
Near Salina, Utah. Utah
Archeology, Vol. 1, No. 4,
pp. 3-7. Salt Lake City.

1957   Two Fremont Sites and Their
Position in Southwestern Prehistory. University of Utah
Anthropological Papers, No.
29. Salt Lake City.

1970   Classical Fremont. Paper presented at the Fremont Culture
Symposium, Society for American Archaeology Meeting, May
1970, Mexico City.

THOMPSON, RICHARD A.

1975a   An Archeological Survey in the
Escalante Valley of Western
Beaver County, Utah. MS,
Department of Anthropology,
University of Utah. Salt Lake
City.

1975b   A Report of Archeological Sur-
veys in the Dry Valley, Henri-
ville, and Alvey Wash Seeding
Areas. MS, Department of
Anthropology, University of
Utah. Salt Lake City.

1976a   The Archeology of the Virgin
Branch of the Kayenta Anasazi:
A Bibliography. MS, Department
of Anthropology, University of
Utah. Salt Lake City.

1976b   The GKS Project: A Limited
Archeological Survey in the
Escalante Valley of Western
Iron County, Utah. MS, Depart-
ment of Anthropology, Univer-
sity of Utah. Salt Lake City.

THOMPSON, RICHARD A., and GEORGIA BETH
THOMPSON

1974*   An Archeological Survey of the
Eastern End of the Warner Valley, Washington County, Utah.
MS, Southern Utah State College. Cedar City.

THOMPSON, WILLIAM L.

1959*   Report of Archeological Reconnaissance of Fable Valley,
Utah. Desert.

TOBIN, SAMUEL J.

1947a   Field Studies in Southwestern
Colorado. MA thesis, Department
of Anthropology, University of
Utah. Salt Lake City.

1947b   Archeology in the San Juan.
University of Utah Anthropo-
logical Papers, No. 8. Salt
Lake City.

TRIPP, GEORGE W.

1963a   Unusual Historical Indian
Burial. Utah Archeology, Vol.
9, No. 3, pp. 1-2. Salt Lake
City.

1963b   Manti Mystery. Utah Archeology,
Vol. 9, No. 4, pp. 1-2. Salt
Lake City.

1964   Authentic Clovis Point Find.
Utah Archeology, Vol. 10, No.
4, p. 1. Salt Lake City.

1966   A Clovis Point from Central
        Utah. American Antiquity, Vol.
        31, No. 3, pp. 435-36. Washing-
        ton, D.C.

1967a   An Unusual Split Willow Figur-
        ine Found Near Green River,
        Utah. Utah Archeology, Vol.
        13, No. 1, p. 15. Salt Lake
        City.

1967b   Bill Mobely does it again!
        Utah Archeology, Vol. 13, No.
        1, p. 16. Salt Lake City.

1967c   A Mountain Sheep Skull Exhi-
        biting Unusual Modifications.
        Utah Archeology, Vol. 13, No.
        2, pp. 4-7. Salt Lake City.

TROUP, TERI

1976*   Tree-ring dating of Anasazi
        Culture at Natural Bridges
        National Monument. MS,
        Natural Bridges National
        Monument.

TURNER, CHRISTY G., II

1960a   Appendix I: Infant Burials
        from the Catfish Canyon Site.
        In "1958 Excavations, Glen
        Canyon Area," William D. Lipe.
        University of Utah Anthropo-
        logical Papers, No. 44, Glen
        Canyon Series, No. 11, pp.
        233-38. Salt Lake City.

1960b   Appendix II: Husteds Well
        Skeleton. In "1959 Excava-
        tions, Glen Canyon Area,"
        William D. Lipe, et al. Uni-
        versity of Utah Anthropolo-
        gical Papers, No. 49, Glen
        Canyon Series, No. 13, pp.
        237-38. Salt Lake City.

1960c* The Location of Human Skele-
        tons Excavated from Prehis-
        toric Sites in the Southwes-
        tern United States. Museum
        of Northern Arizona Technical
        Series, No. 3. Flagstaff.

1960d   Mystery Canyon Survey: San
        Juan County, Utah, 1959.
        Plateau, Vol. 32, No. 4,
        pp. 73-80. Flagstaff.

1961a   Appendix II: Human Skeletons
        from the Coombs Site: Skeletal
        and Dental Aspects. In "The
        Coombs Site, Part III, Summary
        and Conclusions," Robert H.
        Lister and Florence C. Lister.
        University of Utah Anthropolo-
        gical Papers, No. 41, Glen
        Canyon Series, No. 8, pp. 117-
        36. Salt Lake City.

1961b   Appendix III: Human Skeletal
        Material. In "1960 Excavations,
        Glen Canyon Area," Floyd W.
        Sharrock, et al. University of
        Utah Anthropological Papers,
        No. 52, Glen Canyon Series,
        No. 14, pp. 338-60. Salt Lake
        City.

1962a   Further Baldrock Crescent
        Explorations, San Juan County,
        Utah, 1960. Plateau, Vol. 34,
        No. 4, pp. 101-112. Flagstaff.

1962b* A Summary of the Archaeologi-
        cal Explorations of Dr. Byron
        Cummings in the Anasazi Cul-
        ture Area. Museum of Northern
        Arizona Technical Series, No.
        5. Flagstaff.

1963   Petrographs of the Glen Canyon
        Region: The Styles, Chronology,
        Distribution, and Relation-
        ships from Basketmaker to
        Navajo. Museum of Northern
        Arizona Bulletin, No. 38,
        Glen Canyon Series, No. 4.
        Flagstaff.

1966   ABO(H) Antigen Tests on Indian
        Skeletons from Lapoint, Utah.
        In "Caldwell Village," J.
        Richard Ambler. University of
        Utah Anthropological Papers,
        No. 84, pp. 93-96. Salt Lake
        City.

TURNER, CHRISTY G., II, and MAURICE E. COOLEY

1960   Prehistoric Use of Stone from the Glen Canyon Region. Plateau, Vol. 33, No. 2, pp. 46–53. Flagstaff.

UMSHLER, DENNIS

1975   Sources of the Evans Mound Obsidian. MS, Department of Anthropology, University of Utah. Salt Lake City.

UNIVERSITY OF COLORADO MUSEUM

n.d.*   Report of Archeological Research in the Yampa and Green River Canyons, Dinosaur National Monument and Adjacent Areas, 1950. MS, Midwest Archeological Center. Lincoln.

UPPER COLORADO RIVER COMMISSION

1963   Colorado River Storage Project Progress Report. MS, Department of Anthropology, University of Utah. Salt Lake City.

VAN GERVEN, DENNIS P., and JAMES H. MIELKE

1968   Analysis of Two Skeletons from Pharo Village. In "Pharo Village," John P. Marwitt. University of Utah Anthropological Papers, No. 91, pp. 73–78. Salt Lake City.

WALKER, J. TERRY

1977*   Archeological Investigations on Trough Springs Ridge and near the Huntington Canyon – Electric Lake Dam. MS, Department of Anthropology, Brigham Young University. Provo.

WAUER, ROLAND

1965   Pictograph Site in Cave Valley, Zion National Park, Utah. University of Utah Anthropological Papers, No. 75, Miscellaneous Collected Papers, No. 9. Salt Lake City.

WEDEL. W.

1967   Review of Aikens, "Fremont-Promontory-Plains Relationships in Northern Utah." American Journal of Archeology, Vol. 71, No. 4, pp. 426–27. New York.

WELLER, TED

1959   San Juan Triangle Survey. In "The Glen Canyon Archeological Survey, Part II," Don D. Fowler, et al. University of Utah Anthropological Papers, No. 39, Glen Canyon Series, No. 6, pp. 543–675. Salt Lake City.

WELTFISH, GENE

1932a   Problems in the Study of Ancient and Modern Basketmakers. American Anthropologist, n.s. Vol. 34, No. 1, pp. 108–117. Washington, D.C.

1932b   Preliminary Classification of Prehistoric Southwestern Basketry. Smithsonian Miscellaneous Collections, Vol. 87, No. 7. Washington, D.C.

WETHERILL, BEN W.

1934*   Summary of Investigations by the Zion National Park Archaeological Party. Zion and Bryce Nature Notes, Vol. 6, No. 1, pp. 1–9. Zion National Park.

1935*   General Report of the Archaeological Work. Rainbow Bridge--Monument Valley Expedition, Preliminary Bulletin, Archaeological Series, No. 5.

WHEELER, EDWARD A.

1968   An Archeological Survey of West Canyon and Vicinity, Utah County, Utah. MA thesis, Department of Anthropology, Brigham Young University. Provo.

WHEELER, G.M.

1874   Progress Report upon Geograph-
        ical and Geological Explora-
        tions and Surveys West of the
        100th Meridian, in 1872.
        Washington, D.C.

1889   Report on United States Geo-
        graphical Surveys West of the
        100th Meridian, Vol. 1.
        Washington, D.C.

WHEELER, S.M.

1938*   A Fremont Moccasin from Nevada.
        The Masterkey, Vol. 12, No. 1,
        pp. 34-35. Los Angeles.

WHITING, A.F.

1939   Ethnobotany of the Hopi.
        Museum of Northern Arizona
        Bulletin, No. 15. Flagstaff.

WIKLE, LES

1976   Lithic Artifacts of Montezuma
        Canyon: An Inventory and a
        Cultural Application. MA
        thesis, Department of Anthro-
        pology, Brigham Young Univer-
        sity. Provo.

WILSON, CURTIS J.

1972   Ground Stone. In "The Evans
        Site," Michael S. Berry. A
        Special Report. Department of
        Anthropology, University of
        Utah. Salt Lake City.

(ED.)

1974   Highway U-95 Archeology: Comb
        Wash to Grand Flat, Vol. II.
        A Special Report. Department
        of Anthropology, University of
        Utah. Salt Lake City.

WILSON, CURTIS J., and HOWARD L. SMITH

1975   Interstate Highway I-70 Sal-
        vage Archeology, 1974. Anti-
        quities Section Selected

Papers, Vol. 2, No. 7. Utah
State Historical Society,
Salt Lake City.

WINTCH, LEONA FETZER

1963   Extension of Black Fork Cul-
        ture Materials. Utah Archeo-
        logy, Vol. 9, No. 3, pp. 2-9.
        Salt Lake City.

WINTER, JOSEPH C.

1971a   Floral Associations of the
        Clydes Cavern Area. MS, De-
        partment of Anthropology,
        University of Utah. Salt
        Lake City.

1971b   Corn from Clydes Cavern. In
        Report of Excavations at
        Clydes Cavern (42Em177), Emery
        County, Utah, Henry C. Wylie.
        MS, Department of Anthropology,
        University of Utah. Salt Lake
        City.

1972   Evans Mound Cultigens and the
        Fremont Maize Complex. In
        "The Evans Site," Michael S.
        Berry. A Special Report.
        Department of Anthropology,
        University of Utah. Salt Lake
        City.

1973a   The Distribution and Develop-
        ment of Fremont Maize Agri-
        culture: Some Preliminary
        Interpretations. American
        Antiquity, Vol. 38, No. 4,
        pp. 439-52. Washington, D.C.

1973b   The Center Beam Site. In
        "Highway U-95 Archeology:
        Comb Wash to Grand Flat,"
        Gardiner F. Dalley (ed.). A
        Special Report. Department of
        Anthropology, University of
        Utah. Salt Lake City.

1974a   The Arrival and Spread of
        Maize Farming in the Prehis-
        toric Southwest. MS, Department
        of Anthropology, University of
        Utah. Salt Lake City.

1974b   Aboriginal Agriculture in the Southwest and Great Basin. Ph.D. dissertation, Department of Anthropology, University of Utah. Salt Lake City.

1974c   Hovenweep 1974. San Jose State University Archeological Report, No. 1. San Jose.

1974d   The Hovenweep Archaeological Project: A Study of Aboriginal Agriculture. Southwestern Lore, Vol. 40, Nos. 3-4, pp. 23-28. Boulder.

1975a   Hovenweep 1975. San Jose State University Archeological Report, No. 2. San Jose.

1975b*   Preliminary Report: Hovenweep 1975. A Special Report. Department of Anthropology, San Jose State University. San Jose.

1976a   Hovenweep 1976: Preliminary Report. San Jose State University Archeological Report, No. 3. San Jose.

1976b   The Processes of Farming Diffusion in the Southwest and Great Basin. American Antiquity, Vol. 41, No. 4, pp. 421-29. Washington, D.C.

1977   Maize from Backhoe Village and its Relations with the Fremont/Sevier Corn Complex. In "Backhoe Village," David B. Madsen, and LaMar W. Lindsay. Antiquities Section Selected Papers, Vol. 4, No. 12, pp. 105-114. Utah State Historical Society, Salt Lake City.

n.d.   Corn from Cowboy Cave. In "Cowboy Cave," Jesse D. Jennings. University of Utah Anthropological Papers, in preparation. Salt Lake City.

WINTER, JOSEPH C., and HENRY G. WYLIE

1974   Paleoecology and Diet at Clyde's Cavern. American Antiquity, Vol. 39, No. 2, pp. 303-315. Washington, D.C.

WOODBURY, ANGUS

1965   Notes on the Human Ecology of Glen Canyon. University of Utah Anthropological Papers, No. 74, Glen Canyon Series, No. 26. Salt Lake City.

WOODBURY, ANGUS, et al.

1959   Ecological Studies of the Flora and Fauna in Glen Canyon. University of Utah Anthropological Papers, No. 40, Glen Canyon Series, No. 7. Salt Lake City.

WOODBURY, RICHARD B.

1954   Prehistoric Stone Implements of Northeastern Arizona. Peabody Museum of American Archaeology and Ethnology, Harvard University, Papers, No. 34. Cambridge.

1962   Civilizations in Desert Lands. University of Utah Anthropological Papers, No. 62. Salt Lake City.

WORMINGTON, H. MARIE

1948   Preliminary Report on Excavations at the Turner Site in Eastern Utah. Southwestern Lore, Vol. 14, No. 2, pp. 23-24. Boulder.

1955   A Reappraisal of the Fremont Cultures with a Summary of the Archeology of the Northern Periphery. Denver Museum of Natural History Proceedings, No. 1. Denver.

1956   Prehistoric Indians of the Southwest. 3rd edition. <u>Denver Museum of Natural History, Popular Series</u>, No. 7. Denver.

1957   Ancient Man in North America. 4th edition. <u>Denver Museum of Natural History, Popular Series</u>, No. 4. Denver.

WORMINGTON, H. MARIE, and R.H. LISTER

1956   Archeological Investigations on the Uncompahgre Plateau in West Central Colorado. <u>Denver Museum of Natural History, Proceedings</u>, No. 2. Denver.

WORTHINGTON, C. ANNE

1977*   <u>Archeological Research of the Henry Mountains Resource Area</u>. MS, Western Interstate Commission for Higher Education. Boulder.

WYLIE, HENRY G.

1970   <u>Archeological Reconnaissance of Northwestern Utah and Northeastern Nevada, First Season</u>. MS, Department of Anthropology, University of Utah. Salt Lake City.

1971a   <u>Archeological Reconnaissance of Northwestern Utah and Northeastern Nevada, Second Season</u>. MS, Department of Anthropology, University of Utah. Salt Lake City.

1971b   <u>Summary and Recommendations upon Archeological Reconnaissance of Northwestern Utah and Northeastern Nevada</u>. MS, Department of Anthropology, University of Utah. Salt Lake City.

1971c   Report of Excavations at Clyde's Cavern (42Em177), Emery County, Utah. <u>A Special Report</u>. Department of Anthropology, University of Utah. Salt Lake City.

1973   <u>Microanalysis and Functional Typology of the Hogup Cave Chipped Stone Tools</u>. MA thesis, Department of Anthropology, University of Utah. Salt Lake City.

1974   Promontory Pegs as Elements of Great Basin Subsistence Technology. <u>Tebiwa</u>, Vol. 16, No. 2, pp. 46-68. Pocatello.

1975a   Pot Scrapers and Drills from Southern Utah. <u>The Kiva</u>, Vol. 40, No. 3, pp. 121-30. Tucson.

1975b   Tool Microwear and Functional Types from Hogup Cave, Utah. <u>Tebiwa</u>, Vol. 17, No. 2, pp. 1-32. Pocatello.

WYLIE, HENRY G., GARDINER F. DALLEY and JAMES ZEIDLER

1971   <u>The Evans Mound: Report, First Season, 1970</u>. MS, Department of Anthropology, University of Utah. Salt Lake City.

YOUNG, LEVI E.

1929*   The Ancient Inhabitants of Utah. <u>Art and Archaeology</u>, Vol. 27, No. 3, pp. 124-35.

ZALUCHA, L. ANTHONY

1976a* <u>Trip Report and Archeological Assessment, Hall's Crossing Access Road Construction Area, GLCA Area</u>. Report, Midwest Archeological Center. Lincoln.

1976b* <u>Archeological Survey, Dinosaur Quarry Locale, Dinosaur National Monument</u>. Report, Midwest Archeological Center. Lincoln.

ZEIDLER, JAMES A.

1972   <u>An Inventory of Utah's Archeological Resources</u>. MS, Department of Anthropology, University of Utah. Salt Lake City.

1973   The Lizard Ridge Site. In
        "Highway U-95 Archeology:
        Comb Wash to Grand Flat,"
        Gardiner F. Dalley (ed.).
        A Special Report, pp. 75-96.
        Department of Anthropology,
        University of Utah. Salt
        Lake City.

ZINGG, ROBERT M.

  1938* The Ute Indians in Historical
         Relation to Proto-Azteco-
         Tanoan Culture. Colorado
         Magazine, July, pp. 1-19.

  1939   A Reconstruction of Uto-
         Aztekan History. University
         of Denver Contributions to
         Ethnography, No. 2. Denver.